S. HRG. 109–948

ISLAM AND THE WEST: SEARCHING FOR COMMON GROUND

I0439818

HEARING

BEFORE THE

COMMITTEE ON FOREIGN RELATIONS UNITED STATES SENATE

ONE HUNDRED NINTH CONGRESS

SECOND SESSION

JULY 18, 2006

Printed for the use of the Committee on Foreign Relations

Available via the World Wide Web: http://www.gpoaccess.gov/congress/index.html

U.S. GOVERNMENT PRINTING OFFICE

36–963 PDF   WASHINGTON : 2007

For sale by the Superintendent of Documents, U.S. Government Printing Office
Internet: bookstore.gpo.gov Phone: toll free (866) 512–1800; DC area (202) 512–1800
Fax: (202) 512–2250 Mail: Stop SSOP, Washington, DC 20402–0001

COMMITTEE ON FOREIGN RELATIONS

RICHARD G. LUGAR, Indiana, *Chairman*

CHUCK HAGEL, Nebraska
LINCOLN CHAFEE, Rhode Island
GEORGE ALLEN, Virginia
NORM COLEMAN, Minnesota
GEORGE V. VOINOVICH, Ohio
LAMAR ALEXANDER, Tennessee
JOHN E. SUNUNU, New Hampshire
LISA MURKOWSKI, Alaska
MEL MARTINEZ, Florida

JOSEPH R. BIDEN, JR., Delaware
PAUL S. SARBANES, Maryland
CHRISTOPHER J. DODD, Connecticut
JOHN F. KERRY, Massachusetts
RUSSELL D. FEINGOLD, Wisconsin
BARBARA BOXER, California
BILL NELSON, Florida
BARACK OBAMA, Illinois

KENNETH A. MYERS, Jr., *Staff Director*
ANTONY J. BLINKEN, *Democratic Staff Director*

(II)

CONTENTS

(III)

ISLAM AND THE WEST: SEARCHING FOR COMMON GROUND

TUESDAY, JULY 18, 2006

U.S. SENATE,
COMMITTEE ON FOREIGN RELATIONS,
Washington, DC.

The committee met, pursuant to notice, at 10:00 a.m., in room SD–419, Dirksen Senate Office Building, Hon. Richard G. Lugar (chairman of the committee) presiding.

Present: Senators Lugar and Boxer.

OPENING STATEMENT OF HON. RICHARD G. LUGAR, U.S. SENATOR FROM INDIANA

The CHAIRMAN. This hearing of the Foreign Relations Committee is called to order. The committee meets today to convene the second in a series of hearings on the issue of global terrorism and our national and international efforts to combat it.

The issue regrettably remains very much in the headlines. Just last week commuters in Bombay experienced the spontaneous and tragic consequences of terrorism. As tensions flare and more lives are lost in the volatile Middle East, terrorist acts continue to be a tactic of those wishing to achieve political objectives.

In our first hearing we heard from both current and former senior Government officials on the state of the terrorist threat against the United States, and we received recommendations for measuring success and moving forward. We learned that while there have been unequivocal successes in our war against terror, the root causes of terrorism, particularly those driven by Islamic radicalism, remain very much with us.

I noted during our last hearing that military operations alone will not win the longer war on terrorism, and this view was validated by testimony at the hearing. Even with an al-Qaeda organization that is scattered and on the run, its leadership continues to provide ideological guidance to followers worldwide. In other words, despite our operational and tactical successes on several fronts, the root causes of terrorism and the intense ideological motivation behind this phenomenon persist.

We have started this inquiry from the premise that the United States antiterrorism strategy cannot be reduced to military terms or to a fight against existing conspirators. It must include longer-term measures designed to prevent terrorist cells and movements that would target Americans on our shores and abroad from forming in the first place. In today's world, an antiterrorist strategy cannot focus exclusively on "capture and kill" or on the derailment of imminent terrorist acts. Terrorism is a complex phenomenon that requires the application of technological, military, law enforcement, economic, diplomatic, and moral resources.

To evaluate the United States' antiterrorism strategy, we have to know what causes a person to embrace an ideology that would have them resort to terrorism as a tactic. And once inclined toward such ideology, what is it that would dissuade a person from committing violence toward Americans in the first place?

Congressional oversight should ensure that we are getting the maximum benefit out of our antiterrorism investments, that agencies are working cooperatively and effectively with one another, and that we are implementing a comprehensive strategy focused on achievable short- and long-term objectives. And, finally, we must know how we can define our success in this effort and how we would know when we have achieved it.

The purpose of today's hearing is to perform an examination of the historical roots of terrorism and how other nations have dealt with the phenomenon. We will focus in particular on the roots of Islamic-based terrorism, including the current image of the United States in the Muslim world, how Westerners and Muslims view each other, and the state of the struggle within contemporary Islam between its more moderate and extreme factions. We will also probe how the United States and its Western allies and counterparts can move toward a more productive, longer-term relationship with the Muslim world.

Our panel today consists of four individuals who have unique experience to inform us on this complex and important topic.

Dr. Bruce Hoffman is the corporate chair in counterterrorism and counterinsurgency at the RAND Corporation. He is also director of RAND's Washington office. He has a long history of scholarly writing on all aspects of terrorism and counterinsurgency, and has worked as a senior advisor to many government entities in both the United States and Great Britain. He is the editor of "Studies in Conflict and Terrorism," the leading worldwide scholarly journal in the field, and has written extensively on al-Qaeda's tactics, strategies, and leadership.

Mr. Andrew Kohut is the president of the Pew Research Center. He also acts as the director of the Pew Research Center for the People and the Press, and the Pew Global Attitudes Project. He was president of the Gallup organization from 1979 to 1989. Mr. Kohut is widely sought after as a commentator on public opinion and has received many awards in his profession. He is the author of several books, the most recent of which is "America Against the World—How We Are Different and Why We Are Disliked."

Ambassador Akbar Ahmed is a respected scholar on contemporary Islam. He is a former high commissioner of Pakistan to Great Britain, and has advised many world leaders in Islam. He holds a chair in Islamic Studies and is a professor of international relations at American University. The Ambassador is also a distinguished anthropologist, writer, and filmmaker, and is the author of many books on Muslim history and society. He has just returned from an extensive trip throughout the Muslim world.

Dr. Muktedar Khan is a professor of political science and international relations at the University of Delaware, and a nonresident fellow at the Saban Center for Middle East policy at the Brookings Institution. He is known best for his insight relating to the role of moderate Muslims in Islamic thought. His thoughtful post-September 11 essay to his fellow American Muslims has been widely recognized and published. New York Newsday noted that Dr. Khan is "one of a growing number of young moderate Muslim thinkers who believe themselves engaged in a battle for the soul of Islam."

Gentlemen, we welcome you all. We appreciate your willingness to share your thoughts with us today. We look forward to your testimony. Let me mention that your statements will be made a part of the record in full, and I ask for permission that this occur. You may as you choose present your full material, or summarize it. We are here to hear you today, and then hopefully you will respond to our questions.

I would like to recognize the presence of my distinguished colleague from California, Senator Barbara Boxer. Do you have a word of welcome for the witnesses?

Senator BOXER. I do, and I won't give an opening statement. I'm very anxious to hear from them.

But I do welcome you. I think in light of events around the world right now, we need understanding, we need ideas, and we look to you for all of that and more. Thank you.

The CHAIRMAN. Thank you very much, Senator Boxer.

I'll ask you to testify in this order: First of all, Dr. Hoffman, and then Mr. Kohut, and then Mr. Ahmed, and finally Dr. Khan. Would you please proceed, Dr. Hoffman.

STATEMENT OF DR. BRUCE HOFFMAN, CORPORATE CHAIR IN COUNTERTERRORISM AND COUNTERINSURGENCY, THE RAND CORPORATION, WASHINGTON, DC

Dr. HOFFMAN. Thank you, Mr. Chairman. I appreciate very much the opportunity to speak before the committee today on this very important topic.

In your opening remarks you described al-Qaeda as an organization scattered and on the run. My testimony will argue that while that might even recently have been the case, today al-Qaeda has not only regrouped but is in fact on the march.

Let me begin my oral testimony with two brief quotations in the recently cited report by the British parliamentary committee investigating the July 7, 2005 bombings in London:

"We were working off a script which actually has been completely discounted from what we know as reality." That was by Andy Hayman, the assistant commissioner of specialist operations at Scotland Yard, in other words, Britain's top counterterrorism cop.

Second, "I think the more we learned over this period of several years, the more we began to realize the limits of what we knew." This was by Tom Dowse, the chief of the United Kingdom Intelligence Assessments Staff.

These two admissions made by persons at the apex of the United Kingdom's counterterrorism effort encapsulate the central challenge facing the United States today in our own counterterrorism effort. Given the threat's dynamic and evolutionary character and our adversaries' seeming ability to adapt and adjust their tactics and modi operandi to overcome or obviate even our most consequential countermeasures, how can we best ensure that our own assessments and analyses are anchored firmly to sound, empirical judgment and not blinded by either conjecture, mirror-imaging, politically partisan prisms, or wishful thinking? And equally critically, how can we ensure that our counterterrorism policy is sufficiently comprehensive, well-crafted, and effectively directed?

Let me first begin with a brief description of al-Qaeda today, its evolution, adaptation, and adjustment. Al-Qaeda's obituary has been written often since 9/11. Today it is frequently spoken of as an organization in retreat, a broken and beaten movement, incapable of mounting further attacks on its own, and instead having devolved operational authority either to its various affiliates or associates or to entirely organically produced, homegrown terrorist entities. Nothing could be further from the truth.

Al-Qaeda, in fact, is on the march. It has regrouped and reorganized from the setbacks meted out by the United States and our coalition partners and allies during the initial phases of the global war on terrorism, and is marshalling its forces to continue the epic struggle begun now 10 years ago this coming August. The al-Qaeda of today combines, as it always has, both a bottom-up approach, encouraging independent thought and action from low- or lower-level operatives, and a top-down one, with its remaining central command issuing orders and still coordinating a far-flung terrorist enterprise with both highly synchronized and autonomous moving parts.

The most salient threat continues to come from al-Qaeda central and from its affiliates and associated terrorist groups. However, an additional and equally challenging threat is now posed by less discernible and more unpredictable entities drawn from the vast Muslim diaspora and community in Europe. This new category of terrorist adversary, moreover, also has proven more difficult for the authorities in these countries to track, predict, and anticipate. It is also difficult, if not impossible, to effectively profile this adversary.

Indeed, this was precisely the conclusion reached by the abovementioned parliamentary committee in their report on last year's London bombings. Although the members of these terrorist cells may be marginalized individuals working in menial jobs, from the lower socioeconomic strata of society, some with long criminal records or histories of juvenile delinquency, others may well come from solidly middle and upper middle class backgrounds, with university and perhaps even graduate degrees, and prior passions for cars, sports, rock music, and other completely secular material interests.

These new recruits are the anonymous cogs in the worldwide al-Qaeda enterprise, and include both longstanding residents and new immigrants found across Europe, but specifically in countries with large Muslim populations, such as Britain, Spain, France, Germany, Italy, the Netherlands, and Belgium.

Let me now briefly turn to what I argue are the perils of wishful thinking: al-Qaeda and the 7/7 London bombings. The United Kingdom of course rightly prides itself on decades-long experience and detailed knowledge of effectively countering a variety of terrorist threats. Yet, despite Britain's formidable counterterrorist capabilities and unrivaled expertise, its security, intelligence, and law enforcement agencies, as the quotes at the beginning of this testimony evidence, dismissed the likelihood of an imminent attack in the United Kingdom and moreover believed that eventually, when such an attack would occur, it would not involve suicide tactics.

The point of this discussion is most certainly not to criticize our principle ally in the war on terrorism, but rather to highlight the immense difficulties and vast uncertainties concerning countering terrorism today, that have confounded even the enormously professional and experienced British intelligence and security services. Moreover, the danger of similarly cloaking ourselves in a false sense of security based on faulty assumptions or wishful thinking is omnipresent in so fluid and dynamic a terrorism environment as exists today.

Indeed, our appreciation and understanding of the current al-Qaeda threat underscores these perils. Both at the time of the London bombings and since, a misconception has frequently been perpetuated that this was entirely an organic or homegrown phenomena of self-radicalized, self-selected terrorists. Such arguments often were cited in support of the argument that entirely homegrown threats had superseded those posed by al-Qaeda, that al-Qaeda itself was no longer a consequential, active terrorist force, and accordingly that the threat had both changed and perhaps even receded.

The evidence that has come to light since the London attacks a year ago, however, points to the opposite conclusion: That al-Qaeda is not only alive and kicking, but that it is still actively planning and supporting, through the provision of training and perhaps even directing terrorist attacks on a global canvas. Issues of classification and sensitive collection prevent a full description and account of this evidence of active al-Qaeda involvement in the London attacks.

However, suffice it to say that what is publicly known and what has been reported in numerous unclassified sources clearly points to such involvement. Mohammed Siddique Khan, for instance, the ringleader of the London gang, visited Pakistan on at least two occasions, and on his second visit was accompanied by another London bomber, Shazad Tanweer. It is believed that they visited Pakistani jihadi terrorist training camps, and indeed that they met with al-Qaeda operatives.

Both men made "martyrdom" videos while they were in Pakistan between November 2004 and February 2005 and, like all of Osama bin Laden's most important videotaped statements and appearances, the Khan and Tanweer statements were both professionally produced and released by al-Qaeda's perennially active communications department, Al Sahab for Media Production. Al Sahab means "the clouds."

Finally, in concluding my testimony, how do we move toward a new U.S. counterterrorism policy, given the changing and dynamic character of the terrorist threat today? This brief discussion of the 7/7 London bombings is intended to illustrate the dynamic, changing nature of a threat that cannot be defeated by military means alone.

Yet our policy to date has arguably been predominantly weighted toward the tactical "kill and capture" approach in metric, assuming that a traditional center of gravity exists, whether the target is al-Qaeda or the insurgency in Iraq, and that this target simply needs to be destroyed so that global terrorism or the Iraqi insurgency will end. However, both our adversaries today and the threats that they pose are much more elusive and complicated and, as the previous discussion of the London attacks clearly depicts, less neatly amenable to kinetic solutions.

Accordingly, a new strategy and a new approach is vital. Its success will be predicated upon a strategy that effectively combines the tactical elements of systematically destroying and weakening enemy capabilities—the "kill/capture" approach—alongside the equally critical, broader strategic imperative of breaking the cycle of terrorist recruitment and replenishment that have respectively sustained both al-Qaeda's continued campaign and the ongoing conflict in Iraq.

A successful strategy will thus be one that also thinks and plans ahead, with a view toward addressing the threats likely to be posed by the terrorist and insurgent generation, not only beyond the current one but beyond the one after the current one. At the foundation of such a dynamic and adaptive strategy must be the ineluctably maxim that effectively and successfully countering terrorism as well as insurgency, is not exclusively a military endeavor, but involves fundamental parallel political, social, economic, and ideological activities.

Accordingly, rather than viewing the fundamental organizing principle of American national defense strategy in this unconventional realm as a global war on terrorism, it may be more useful to reconceptualize it in terms of a global counterinsurgency. Such an approach would, a priori, knit together the equally critical political, economic, diplomatic, and developmental sides inherent to the successful prosecution of counterterrorism and counterinsurgency, and contribute to the existing dominant military side of the equation.

Greater attention to this integration of American capabilities would provide incontrovertible recognition of the importance of endowing a global counterinsurgency with an overriding and comprehensive multidimensional policy. Ideally, this policy would embrace several elements, including a clear strategy, a defined structure for implementing it, and a vision of intergovernmental agency cooperation and a unified effort to guide it. A more focused and strengthened interagency process would also facilitate the coordination of key themes and messages, and the development and execution of long-term "hearts and minds" programs.

The U.S. Government, in sum, will need to adjust and adapt its strategy, resources, and tactics to formidable opponents that, as we have seen, are widely dispersed and decentralized, and whose many destructive parts are autonomous, mobile, and themselves highly adaptive. In this respect, even the best strategy will be proven inadequate if military and civilian agency leaders are not prepared to engage successfully within ambiguous environments and to reorient their organizational culture to deal with irregular threats.

A successful global counterinsurgency transcends the need for better tactical intelligence or new organizations. It is fundamentally about transforming the attitudes and mindsets of leaders so that they have the capacity to take decisive yet thoughtful action against terrorists and insurgents in uncertain or unclear situations, based on a common vision, policy, and strategy.

In sum, new times, new threats, and new challenges make a new strategy, approach, and new organizational and institutional behaviors necessary. The effectiveness of a U.S. strategy will be based on our capacity to think like a networked enemy, in anticipation of how they may act in a variety of situations, aided by different resources.

This goal requires that the American national security structure, in turn, organize itself for maximum efficiency, information-sharing, and the ability to function quickly and effectively under new operational definitions. With this understanding in mind, we need to craft an approach that specifically takes into account the following key factors to effectively wage a global counterinsurgency:

- One, separating the enemy from the populace that provides its support and sustenance. This, in turn, entails three basic missions: denial of enemy sanctuary; elimination of enemy freedom of movement; denial of enemy resources and support.
- Second, identification and neutralization of the enemy.
- Third, creation of a secure environment, progressing from local to regional to global.
- Fourth, ongoing and effective neutralization of enemy propaganda and information operations through the planning and execution of a comprehensive and integrated information operations and holistic civil affairs campaign of our own.
- Finally, interagency efforts to build effective and responsible civil governance mechanisms that eliminate the fundamental causes of terrorism and insurgency.

In conclusion, al-Qaeda may be compared to the archetypal shark in the water that must keep moving forward, no matter how slowly or incrementally, or die. In al-Qaeda's context, this means adapting and adjusting to our countermeasures while simultaneously searching to identify new targets and new vulnerabilities. In this respect, al-Qaeda's capacity to continue to prosecute this struggle is a direct reflection of both the movement's resiliency and the continued resonance of its ideology.

Al-Qaeda's operational durability thus has enormous significance for United States counterterrorism strategy and policy. Because al-Qaeda has this malleable resiliency, it cannot be defeated or destroyed in a single military engagement or even a series of engagements, much less ones exclusively dependent on the application of conventional forces and firepower. To a significant degree, our ability to carry out such missions effectively will depend on the ability of American strategy and policy to adjust and adapt to changes we see in the nature and character of our adversaries. Thank you very much, Mr. Chairman.

[The prepared statement of Mr. Hoffman follows:]

PREPARED STATEMENT OF DR. BRUCE HOFFMAN, CORPORATE CHAIR IN COUNTERTERRORISM AND COUNTERINSURGENCY, RAND CORPORATION, WASHINGTON, DC

"We were working off a script which actually has been completely discounted from what we know as reality."—Andy Hayman, Assistant Commissioner of Specialist Operations, Scotland Yard

"I think the more we learned over this period of several years, the more we began to realize the limits of what we knew . . ."—Tom Dowse, Chief of the Assessments Staff

These two admissions, made by persons at the apex of the United Kingdom's counterterrorism effort, encapsulate the central challenge today facing the United States in our own counterterrorism effort. Given the threat's dynamic and evolutionary character and our adversaries' seeming ability to adapt and adjust their tactics and modi operandi to overcome or obviate even our most consequential countermeasures, how can we best ensure that our own assessments and analyses are anchored firmly to sound, empirical judgment and not blinded by either conjecture, mirror-imaging, politically partisan prisms or wishful thinking? And, equally critically, how can we ensure that our counterterrorism policy is sufficiently comprehensive, well crafted and effectively directed?

AL-QAEDA TODAY: EVOLUTION, ADAPTATION, AND ADJUSTMENT

Al-Qaeda's obituary has been written often since 9/11. "Al-Qa'ida's Top Primed To Collapse, U.S. Says," trumpeted a Washington Post headline 2 weeks after Khalid Sheikh Mohammed, the mastermind behind the 9/11 attacks, was arrested in March 2003. "I believe the tide has turned in terms of al-Qa'ida," Congressmen Porter J. Goss, then-chairman of the U.S. House of Representatives Intelligence Committee and himself a former CIA case officer who became its director a year later, was quoted. "We've got them nailed," an unidentified intelligence expert was quoted, who still more expansively declared, "we're close to dismantling them." These upbeat assessments continued the following month with the nearly bloodless capture of Baghdad and the failure of al-Qaeda to make good on threats of renewed attacks in retaliation for invasion. Citing administration sources, an article in the Washington Times on 24 April 2003 reported the prevailing view in official Washington that al-Qaeda's "failure to carry out a successful strike during the United States-led military campaign to topple Saddam Hussein has raised questions about their ability to carry out major new attacks." Despite major terrorist attacks in Jakarta and Istanbul during the latter half of that same year and the escalating insurgency in Iraq, this optimism carried into 2004. "The al-Qaida of the 9/11 period is under catastrophic stress," Ambassador Cofer Black, at the time the U.S. State Department's Counterterrorism Coordinator, declared. "They are being hunted down, their days are numbered." Then came the Madrid bombings 6 weeks later and the deaths of 191 persons. The most accurate assessment, perhaps, was therefore the one offered by al-Qaeda itself. "The Americans," Thabet bin Qais, a spokesperson for the movement said in May 2003, "only have predications and old intelligence left. It will take them a long time to understand the new form of al-Qaida." Admittedly, while the first part of bin Qais's assertion is not correct, there is more than a grain of truth to the second part. More than 3 years later we are indeed still struggling to understand the changing character and nature of al-Qaeda and the shifting dimensions of the terrorist threat as it has evolved since 9/11.

Today, al-Qaeda is also frequently spoken of as if it is in retreat: A broken and beaten organization, incapable of mounting further attacks on its own and instead having devolved operational authority either to its various affiliates and associates or to entirely organically-produced, homegrown, terrorist entities. Nothing could be further from the truth. Al-Qaeda it has regrouped and reorganized from the setbacks meted out to it by the United States and our coalition partners and allies during the initial phases of the global war on terrorism (GWOT) and is marshalling its forces to continue the epic struggle begun now some 10 years ago. Al-Qaeda is now functioning exactly as its founder and leader, Osama bin Laden envisioned it. On the one hand, true to the meaning of the Arabic word for the "base of operation" or "foundation" meaning the base or foundation from which worldwide Islamic revolution can be waged (or, as other translations have it, the "precept" or "method") and thus simultaneously inspiring, motivating, and animating radicalized Muslims to join the movement's fight. While, on the other, continuing to exercise its core operational and command and control capabilities—directing the implementing terrorist attacks.

The al-Qaeda of today combines, as it always has, both a "bottom up" approach—encouraging independent thought and action from low- (or lower-) level operatives—and a "top down" one—issuing orders and still coordinating a far-flung terrorist enterprise with both highly synchronized and autonomous moving parts. Mixing and matching organizational and operational styles whether dictated by particular missions or imposed by circumstances, the al-Qaeda movement, accordingly, can perhaps most usefully be conceptualized as comprising four distinct, though not mutually exclusive, dimensions. In descending order of sophistication, they are:

- *Al-Qaeda Central.* This category comprises the remnants of the pre-9/11 al-Qaeda organization. Although its core leadership includes some of the familiar, established commanders of the past, there are a number of new players who have advanced through the ranks as a result of the death or capture of key al-Qaeda senior-level managers such as Abu Atef, KSM, and Hambali, and more recently, Abu Faraj al-Libi and Abu Hamza Rabia. It is believed that this hardcore remains centered in or around the Afghanistan and Pakistan borders and continues to exert actual coordination, if not some direct command and control capability, in terms of commissioning attacks, directing surveillance and collating reconnaissance, planning operations, and approving their execution.

This category comes closest to the al-Qaeda operational template or model evident in the 1998 East Africa embassy bombings and 9/11 attacks. Such high value, "spectacular" attacks are entrusted only to al-Qaeda's professional cadre: The most dedicated, committed, and absolutely reliable element of the movement. Previous patterns suggest that these "professional" terrorists are deployed in predetermined and carefully selected teams. They will also have been provided with very specific targeting instructions. In some cases, such as the East Africa bombings, they may establish contact with, and enlist the assistance of, local sympathizers and supporters. This will be solely for logistical and other attack-support purposes or to enlist these locals to actually execute the attack(s). The operation, however, will be planned and directed by the "professional" element with the locals clearly subordinate and playing strictly a supporting role (albeit a critical one).

- *Al-Qaeda Affiliates and Associates.* This category embraces formally established insurgent or terrorist groups that over the years have benefited from bin Laden's largesse and/or spiritual guidance and/or have received training, arms, money, and other assistance from al-Qaeda. Among the recipients of this assistance have been terrorist groups and insurgent forces in Uzbekistan and Indonesia, Morocco and the Philippines, Bosnia and Kashmir, among other places. By supporting these groups, bin Laden's intentions were threefold. First, he sought to co-opt these movements' mostly local agendas and channel their efforts toward the cause of global jihad. Second, he hoped to create a jihadi "critical mass" from these geographically scattered, disparate movements that would one day coalesce into a single, unstoppable force. And, third, he wanted to foster a dependent relationship whereby as a quid pro quo for prior al-Qaeda support, these movements would either undertake attacks at al-Qaeda's behest or provide essential local, logistical, and other support to facilitate strikes by the al-Qaeda "professional" cadre noted above.

This category includes groups such as: al-Ittihad al-Islami (AIAI), the late Abu Musab Zarqawi's al-Qaeda in Mesopotamia (formerly Jamaat al Tawhid wa'l Jihad), Asbat al-Ansar, Ansar al Islam, Islamic Army of Aden, Islamic Movement of Uzbekistan (IMU), Jemaah Islamiya (JI), Libyan Islamic Fighting Group (LIFG), Moro Islamic Liberation Front (MILF), Salafist Group for Call and Combat (GSPC), and the various Kashmiri Islamic groups based in Pakistan—e.g., Harakat ul Mujahidin (HuM), Jaish-e-Mohammed (JeM), Laskar-e-Tayyiba (LeT), and Laskar i Jhangvi (LiJ). Both the number and geographical diversity of these entities is proof of al-Qaeda's continued influence and vitality.

- *Al-Qaeda Locals.* These are dispersed cells of al-Qaeda adherents who have or have had some direct connection with al-Qaeda—no matter how tenuous or evanescent. They appear to fall into two subcategories.

One category comprises persons who have had some prior terrorism experience—having been blooded in battle as part of some previous jihadi campaign in Algeria, the Balkans, Chechnya, and perhaps more recently in Iraq, and may have trained in some al-Qaeda facility whether in Afghanistan or Yemen or the Sudan before 9/11. Specific examples of this adversary include Ahmed Ressam, who was arrested in December 1999 at Port Angeles, Washington State, shortly after he had entered the United States from Canada. Ressam, for instance, had a prior background in terrorism, having belonged to Algeria's Armed Islamic Group (GIA). After being recruited to al-Qaeda, he was provided with a modicum of basic terrorist training in Afghanistan. In contrast to the professional cadre detailed above, however, Ressam was given very nonspecific, virtually open-ended targeting instructions before being dispatched to North America. Also, unlike the well-funded professional cadre, Ressam was given only $12,000 in "seed money" and instructed to raise the rest of his operational funds from petty thievery. He was also told by KSM to recruit members for his terrorist cell from among the expatriate Muslim communities in Canada and the United States. The al-Qaeda operative, Andrew Rowe, a British national and Muslim convert, convicted for his involvement in the 2003 al-Qaeda plot to attack London's Heathrow Airport is another example of this category.

The other category, as is described in the detailed discussion of the 7/7 London attacks below, conforms to the profile of the four British Muslims responsible for the 2005 bombings of mass transit targets in London. In contrast to Ressam and Rowe, none of the four London bombers had previously fought in any of the contemporary, iconic Muslim conflicts (e.g., Algeria, Chechnya, Kashmir, Bosnia, Afghanistan, etc.) nor is there conclusive evidence of their having received any training in an al-Qaeda camp in Afghanistan, Yemen, or the Sudan prior to 9/11. Rather, at least the two ringleaders of the London cell were recruited locally, brought to Pakistan for training and then returned to their homeland with both an attack plan and the knowledge to implement. They recruited others locally as needed, into the cell and undertook a relatively simple, but nonetheless sophisticated and highly consequential attack.

In both the above categories, however, the terrorists will have some link with al-Qaeda. Their current relationship, and communication, with a central al-Qaeda command and control apparatus may be either active or dormant and similarly their targeting choices may either be specifically directed or else entirely left to the cell to decide. The distinguishing characteristic of this category, however, is that there is some previous direct connection of some kind with al-Qaeda.

- *Al-Qaeda Network.* These are home-grown Islamic radicals—from North Africa, the Middle East, and South and Southeast Asia—as well as local converts to Islam mostly living in Europe, Africa, and perhaps Latin America and North America as well, who have no direct connection with al-Qaeda (or any other identifiable terrorist group), but nonetheless are prepared to carry out attacks in solidarity with or support of al-Qaeda's radical jihadi agenda. Like the "al-Qaeda locals" they too are motivated by a shared sense of enmity and grievance felt toward the United States and West, in general, and their host-nations in particular. In this specific instance, however, the relationship with al-Qaeda is more inspirational than actual, abetted by profound rage over the United States' invasion and occupation of Iraq and the oppression of Muslims in Palestine, Kashmir, Chechnya, and elsewhere. Critically, these persons are neither directly members of a known, organized terrorist group nor necessarily even a very cohesive entity unto themselves.

Examples of this category, which comprises small collections of like-minded locals who gravitate toward one to plan and mount terrorist attacks completely independent of any direction provided by al-Qaeda, include the so-called Hofstad Group in the Netherlands, a member of whom (Mohammed Bouyeri) murdered the Dutch filmmaker, Theo Van Gogh, in Amsterdam in November 2004.

The most salient threat posed by the above categories, however, continues to come from al-Qaeda Central and from its affiliates and associates. However, an additional and equally challenging threat is now posed by less discernible and more unpredictable entities drawn from the vast Muslim Diaspora in Europe. As far back as 2001, the Netherlands' intelligence and security service had detected increased terrorist recruitment efforts among Muslim youth living in the Netherlands whom it was previously assumed had been completely assimilated into Dutch society and culture. Thus, representatives of Muslim extremist organizations—including, presumably, al-Qaeda had already succeeded in embedding themselves in, and drawing new sources of support from, receptive elements within established Diaspora communities. In this way, new recruits could be drawn into the movement who likely had not previously come under the scrutiny of local or national law enforcement agencies.

This new category of terrorist adversary, moreover, also has proven more difficult for the authorities in these countries to track, predict, and anticipate. The director of GCHQ (Government Communications Headquarters), Britain's equivalent of our NSA (National Security Agency) admitted this in testimony before a Parliamentary committee investigating the 7/7 attacks. "We had said before July [2005]," Sir David Pepper noted, there are probably groups out there that we do not know anything about, and because we do not know anything about them we do not know how many there are. What happened in July [the 2005 London bombings] was a demonstration that there were [material redacted for security reasons] conspiracies going on about which we essentially knew nothing, and that rather sharpens the perception of how big, if I can use [Secretary of Defense Donald] Rumsfeld's term, the unknown unknown was.

This adversary, comprising hitherto unknown cells, is difficult, if not impossible, to effectively profile. Indeed, this was precisely the conclusion reached by the above-mentioned Parliamentary committee in their report on the London bombings. Although the members of these terrorist cells may be marginalized individuals working in menial jobs from the lower socioeconomic strata of society, some with long criminal records or histories of juvenile delinquency; others may well come from solidly middle and upper-middle class backgrounds with university and perhaps even graduate degrees and prior passions for cars, sports, rock music, and other completely secular, material interests. For example, in the case of radicalized British Muslims, since 9/11 we have seen terrorists of South Asian and North African descent as well as those hailing both from the Middle East and Caribbean. They have included life-long devout Muslims as well as recent converts. Persons from the margins of society who made a living as thieves or from drug dealing and students at the London School of Economics, one of the U.K.'s premiere universities. This was not a sentence. What they will have in common is a combination of a deep commitment to their faith—often recently rediscovered; admiration of bin Laden for the cathartic blow struck against America on 9/11; hatred of the United States and the West; and, a profoundly shared sense of alienation from their host countries. "There appear to be a number of common features to this grooming," the report of the Intelligence and Security Committee of the U.K. House of Commons concluded.

In the early stages, group conversation may be around being a good Muslim and staying away from drugs and crime, with no hint of an extremist agenda. Gradually individuals may be exposed to propaganda about perceived injustices to Muslims across the world with international conflict involving Muslims interpreted as examples of widespread war against Islam; leaders of the Muslim world perceived as corrupt and non-Islamic; with some domestic policies added as "evidence" of a persecuted Islam; and conspiracy theories abounding. They will then move on to what the extremists claim is religious justification for violent jihad in the Quran and the Hadith . . . and—if suicide attacks are the intention—the importance of martyrdom in demonstrating commitment to Islam and the rewards in Paradise for martyrs; before directly inviting an individual to engage in terrorism. There is little evidence of over compulsion. The extremists appear rather to rely on the development of individual commitment and group bonding and solidarity [my emphasis].

These new recruits are the anonymous cogs in the world-wide al-Qaeda enterprise and include both longstanding residents and new immigrants found across in Europe, but specifically in countries with large expatriate Muslim populations such as Britain, Spain, France, Germany, Italy, the Netherlands, and Belgium.

THE PERILS OF WISHFUL THINKING: AL-QAEDA AND THE 7/7 LONDON BOMBINGS

The United Kingdom, of course, rightly prides itself on decades-long experience and detailed knowledge of effectively countering a variety of terrorist threats. Over the past dozen years the U.K. homeland itself has been subject to attack from a diversity of adversaries including: the Provisional Irish Republican Army, renegade Palestinian factions, and both before and since 9/11 by al-Qaeda as well. Yet, despite Britain's formidable counterterrorist capabilities and unrivaled expertise, only a month before the 7 July 2005 London bombings, the Joint Terrorism Assessment Center (JTAC), the British counterpart of our own NCTC (National Counterterrorism Center) concluded that, "at present there is not a group with both the current intent and the capability to attack in the U.K." and consequently downgraded the overall threat level for the U.K.

More astonishing perhaps was the dismissal of the prospect of suicide terrorist attacks occurring in the United Kingdom, despite the emerging global pattern of terrorism in this respect and the involvement of several British nationals in both attempted and successful suicide attacks elsewhere. Seventy-eight percent of all the suicide terrorist incidents perpetrated between 1968 and 2004, for instance, have occurred in the years following 9/11. And, the dominant force behind this trend is religion—specifically groups and individuals identifying themselves as Islamic. Indeed, of the 35 terrorist organizations currently employing suicide tactics, 86 percent (31 of 35) are Islamic. These movements, moreover, have been responsible for 81 percent of all suicide attacks since 9/11. Indeed, to date, suicide attacks have taken place in at least two dozen countries—including the United Kingdom, Israel, Sri Lanka, Russia, Lebanon, Turkey, Italy, Indonesia, Pakistan, Colombia, Argentina, Kenya, Tanzania, Croatia, Morocco, Singapore, the Philippines, Saudi Arabia, Kuwait, and

Iraq. By comparison, at the dawn of the modern era of religious terrorism some 20 years ago, this was a phenomenon confined exclusively to two countries: Lebanon and Kuwait, and employed by less than a half dozen groups. Yet, only 4 months before the 7/7 bombings, the Joint Intelligence Committee (JIC), Britain's most senior intelligence assessment and evaluation body (one roughly similar to the American intelligence community's NIC, or National Intelligence Center), judged that "such attacks would not become the norm within Europe." This judgment, coupled with the testimony of Dame Eliza Manningham-Buller, the Director-General of the Security Service (MI–5), prompted the aforementioned Parliamentary committee to conclude that "The fact that there were suicide attacks in the U.K. on 7 July was clearly unexpected. The Director General of the Security Service said it was a surprise that the first big attack in the U.K. for 10 years was a suicide attack."

The point of this discussion is most certainly not to criticize our principal ally in the war on terrorism but rather to highlight the immense difficulties and vast uncertainties concerning countering terrorism today that have confounded even the enormously professional and experienced British intelligence and security services. Moreover, the danger of similarly cloaking ourselves in a false sense of security based on faulty assumptions or wishful thinking is omnipresent in so fluid and dynamic a terrorism environment as exists today. Indeed, our appreciation and understanding of the current al-Qaeda threat further underscores these perils. Both at the time of the London bombing attacks and since a misconception has frequently been perpetuated that this was entirely an organic or homegrown phenomenon of self-radicalized, self-selected terrorists. Such arguments often were cited in support of the argument that entirely homegrown threats had superseded those posed of al-Qaeda; that al-Qaeda itself was no longer a consequential, active terrorist force; and accordingly that the threat had both changed and perhaps even receded. The evidence that has come to light since the London attacks a year ago, however, points to the opposite conclusion: That al-Qaeda is not only alive and kicking, but that it is still actively planning, supporting through the provision of training, and perhaps even directing terrorist attacks on a global canvas.

Issues of classification and sensitive collection prevent a full description and account of this evidence of active al-Qaeda involvement in the London attacks. However, suffice it to say that what is publicly known and has been reported in unclassified sources, clearly points to such involvement. For instance, the aforementioned report by the Parliament's Intelligence and Security Committee, noted among its other conclusions, that:

- "Investigations since July have shown that the group [the four London bombers] was in contact with others involved in extremism in the U.K. . . ."
- "Siddique Khan [the group's ringleader] is now known to have visited Pakistan in 2003 and to have spent several months there with Shazad Tanweer [another bomber] between November 2004 and February 2005. It has not yet been established who they met in Pakistan, but it is assessed as likely that they had some contact with al-Qaida figures."
- "The extent to which the 7 July attacks were externally planned, directed, or controlled by contacts in Pakistan or elsewhere remains unclear. The [British intelligence and security] Agencies believe that some form of operational training is likely to have taken place while Khan and Tanweer were in Pakistan. Contacts in the run-up to the attacks suggest they may have had advice or direction from individuals there."

More compelling, albeit for the moment necessarily circumstantial, evidence may be found in the "martyrdom" videos made by Khan and Tanweer sometime while they were in Pakistan between November 2004 and February 2005. Like all Osama bin Laden's most important video taped statements and appearances, the Khan and Tanweer statements were both professionally produced and released by al-Qaeda's perennially-active communications department, "Al Sahab [the Clouds] for Media Production."

The first of the two videos of Khan was broadcast on the Qatar-based Arabic-language news station, al Jazeera, on 1 September 2005. It is worth exploring the content of Khan's statement in some detail since it accurately encapsulates the essence of European Muslim radicalism today. Kahn's statement is especially noteworthy for the following reasons:

- He professes his preeminent allegiance to and identification with his religion and the umma—the worldwide Muslim community. Hence, unlike most Western conceptions of identity and allegiance that are rooted to the nation or state, Khan's is exclusively to a theology.

- Like all terrorists before him, Khan frames his choice of tactic and justifies his actions in ineluctably defensive terms. He describes his struggle as an intrinsically defensive one and his act as a response to the repeated depredations and unmitigated aggression of the West that have been directed against Muslims worldwide.
- The sense of individual empowerment and catharsis evident in Khan's words and demeanor.
- The intense desire for vengeance and martyrdom, with the latter regarded by him as "supreme evidence" of his religious commitment.
- Khan's laudatory comments about bin Laden and his deputy, Ayman al-Zawahiri.

The relevant portions of Khan's statement are as follows:

- I and thousands like me are forsaking everything for what we believe. Our driving motivation doesn't come from tangible commodities that this world has to offer. Our religion is Islam—obedience to the one true God, Allah, and following the footsteps of the final prophet and messenger Muhammad . . . This is how our ethical stances are dictated.
- Your democratically elected governments continuously perpetuate atrocities against my people all over the world. And your support of them makes you directly responsible, just as I am directly responsible for protecting and avenging my Muslim brothers and sisters [my emphasis].
- Until we feel security, you will be our targets. And until you stop the bombing, gassing, imprisonment, and torture of my people we will not stop this fight. We are at war and I am a soldier. Now you too will taste the reality of this situation . . . .
- I myself, I make du'a [calling] to Allah . . . to raise me amongst those whom I love like the prophets, the messengers, the martyrs, and today's heroes like our beloved Sheikh Osama Bin Laden, Dr. Ayman al-Zawahiri and Abu Musab al-Zarqawi, and all the other brothers and sisters that are fighting in . . . this cause.

Al-Zawahiri in fact appears at the end of the same tape, praising Khan for having brought the "blessed battle . . . to the enemy's land." In a subsequent video, aired on al Jazeera on 19 September, al-Zawahiri also claimed responsibility for the attacks in the name of al-Qaeda. Only last week, a similar martyrdom tape made by Khan's traveling companion and fellow bomber, Shahzad Tanweer, was released by al Sahab to mark the first anniversary of the London attacks. Titled, "The Final Message of the Knights of the London Raid," it showed Tanweer expressing similar views to those of Khan. "To the non-Muslims of Britain," he begins: You may wonder what you have done to deserve this. You are those who have voted in your government, who in turn have, and still continue to this day, continue to oppress our mothers, children, brothers, and sisters from the east to the west, in Palestine, Afghanistan, Iraq, and Chechnya. Your government has openly supported the genocide of over 150,000 innocent Muslims in Falluja.

You have offered financial and military support to the United States and Israel, in the massacre of our children in Palestine. You are directly responsible for the problems in Palestine, Afghanistan, and Iraq to this day. You have openly declared war on Islam, and are the forerunners in the crusade against the Muslims.

Al-Zawahiri then appears on screen to explain that, "What made Shehzad join the camps of Qaeda Al-Jihad was the oppression carried out by the British in Iraq, Afghanistan, and Palestine. He would often talk about Palestine, about the British support of the Jews, and about their clear injustice against the Muslims." An unidentified narrator then continues: In order to remove this injustice, Shehzad [sic] began training with all his might and devotion. Together with the martyr Siddiq Khan, he received practical and intensive training in how to produce and use explosives, in the camps of Qaeda Al-Jihad. The recruits who join these camps do not have to achieve high averages or to pass entrance exams. All they need is to be zealous for their religion and nation, and to love jihad and martyrdom for the sake of Allah.

The video continues with Tanweer warning "all you British citizens to stop your support to your lying British Government, and to the so-called 'war on terror,' and ask yourselves why would thousands of men be willing to give their lives for the cause of Muslims." Al-Zawahiri also again appears to emphasize how both Khan and Tanweer were "striving for martyrdom, and were hoping to carry out a martyrdom operation. Both of them were very resolute in this." Tanweer then calls upon his fellow British Muslims to rise and fight the "disbelievers, for it is but an obligation made on you by Allah." A statement is then heard from U.S.-born, Muslim convert

Adam Gadahn ("Azzam the American") before concluding with Tanweer threatening that: What you have witnessed now is only the beginning of a series of attacks, which, in shallah, will intensify and continue until you pull all your troops out of Afghanistan and Iraq, until you stop all financial and military support to the United States and Israel, and until you release all Muslim prisoners from Belmarsh, and your other concentration camps. And know that if you fail to comply with this, then know that this war will never stop, and that we are ready to give our lives, one hundred times over, for the cause of Islam. You will never experience peace, until our children in Palestine, our mothers and sisters in Kashmir, and our brothers in Afghanistan and Iraq feel peace.

TOWARD A NEW U.S. COUNTERTERRORISM POLICY

"Could we, could others, could the police have done better? Could we with greater effort, greater imagination, have stopped it? We knew there were risks we were running. We were trying very hard and very fast to enhance our capacity, but even with the wisdom of hindsight I think it is unlikely that we would have done so, with the resources available to us at the time and the other demands placed upon us. I think that position will remain in the foreseeable future. We will continue to stop most of them, but we will not stop all of them."—Dame Eliza Manningham-Buller, Director-General, U.K. Security Service (MI–5)

As this discussion of the 7/7 London bombings has shown, al-Qaeda and the threat it poses cannot be defeated through military means alone. Yet, our policy to date has arguably been predominantly weighted toward the tactical "kill or capture" approach and metric: Assuming that a traditional center of gravity exists whether the target is al-Qaeda or the insurgency in Iraq and that this target simply needs to be destroyed so that global terrorism or the Iraqi insurgency will end. However, both our adversaries today and the threats that they pose, are much more elusive and complicated and, as the previous discussion of the London attacks clearly depicts, less amenable to kinetic solutions. As one U.S. intelligence officer with vast experience in this realm acerbically told to me nearly 2 years ago: "We don't have enough bullets to kill them all." Accordingly, a new strategy and new approach is vital. Its success will be predicated upon a strategy that effectively combines the tactical elements of systematically destroying and weakening enemy capabilities (the "kill or capture" approach) alongside the equally critical, broader strategic imperative of breaking the cycle of terrorist and insurgent recruitment and replenishment that have respectively sustained both al-Qaeda's continued campaign and the ongoing conflict in Iraq. A successful strategy will thus be one that also thinks and plans ahead with a view toward addressing the threats likely to be posed by the terrorist and insurgent generation beyond the current one.

At the foundation of such a dynamic and adaptive strategy must be the ineluctable axiom that effectively and successfully countering terrorism as well as insurgency is not exclusively a military endeavor but also involves fundamental parallel political, social, economic, and ideological activities. This timeless principle of countering insurgency was first defined by Field Marshal Sir Gerald Templer in Malaya more than 50 years ago. "The shooting side of the business is only 25 percent of the trouble and the other 75 percent lies in getting the people of this country behind us," Templer famously wrote in November 1952, responding to a terrorist directive from the previous year that focused on increasing appreciably the "cajolery" of the population. Accordingly, rather than viewing the fundamental organizing principle of American national defense strategy in this unconventional realm as a GWOT, it may be more useful to reconceptualize it in terms of a global counterinsurgency (GCOIN). Such an approach would a priori knit together the equally critical political, economic, diplomatic, and developmental sides inherent to the successful prosecution of counterinsurgency to the existing dominant military side of the equation.

Such a new approach would necessarily be built upon a more integrated, systems approach to a complex problem that is at once operationally durable, evolutionary and elusive in character. Greater attention to this integration of American capabilities would provide incontrovertible recognition of the importance of endowing a GCOIN with an overriding and comprehensive, multi-dimensional policy. Ideally, this policy would embrace several elements including a clear strategy, a defined structure for implementing it, and a vision of intergovernment agency cooperation, and the unified effort to guide it. It would have particular benefit with respect to the gathering and exploitation of "actionable intelligence." By updating and streamlining interagency counterterrorism and counterinsurgency systems and procedures both strategically as well as operationally between the Department of Defense, the Department of State, and the intelligence community, actionable intelligence could likely be acquired, analyzed, and disseminated faster and operations mounted more quickly. A more focused and strengthened interagency process would also facilitate the coordination of key themes and messages and the development and execution of long-term "hearts and minds" programs.

The U.S. Government, in sum, will need to adjust and adapt its strategy, resources, and tactics to formidable opponents that, as we have seen, are widely dispersed and decentralized and whose many destructive parts are autonomous, mobile, and themselves highly adaptive. In this respect, even the best strategy will be proven inadequate if military and civilian agency leaders are not prepared to engage successfully within ambiguous environments and reorient their organizational culture to deal with irregular threats. A successful GCOIN transcends the need for better tactical intelligence or new organizations. It is fundamentally about transforming the attitudes and mindsets of leaders so that they have the capacity to take decisive, yet thoughtful action against terrorists and/or insurgents in uncertain or unclear situations based on a common vision, policy, and strategy. In addition to traditional "hard" military skills of "kill or capture" and destruction and attrition; "soft" skills such as information operations, negotiation, psychology, social and cultural anthropology, foreign area studies, complexity theory, and systems management will become increasingly important in the ambiguous and dynamic environment in which irregular adversaries circulate.

Arguably, by combating irregular adversaries in a more collaborative manner with key relevant civilian agencies, military planners can better share critical information, track the various moving parts in terrorist/insurgency networks, and develop a comprehensive picture of this enemy—including their supporters, nodes of support, organizational and operational systems, processes, and plans. With this information in hand, the United States would then be better prepared to systematically disrupt or defeat all of the critical nodes that support the entire terrorist/insurgent network, thus rendering them ineffective. Achieving this desideratum, however, will necessitate the coordination, deconflicting, and synchronization of the variety of programs upon which the execution of American counterterrorist and/or counterinsurgency planning are dependent. An equally critical dimension of this process will be aligning the training of host nation counterparts with GWOT/GCOIN operations: Building synergy; avoiding duplication of effort; ensuring that training leads to operational effectiveness; and ensuring that the U.S. interagency team and approach is in complete harmony. In other words, aligning these training programs (among the different government agencies) with GCOIN operations to build indigenous capabilities in counterterrorism and counterinsurgency will be absolutely fundamental to the success of such a strategy.

In sum, new times, new threats, and new challenges ineluctably make a new strategy, approach, and new organizational and institutional behaviors necessary. The threat posed by elusive and deadly irregular adversaries emphasizes the need to anchor changes that will more effectively close the gap between detecting irregular adversarial activity and rapidly defeating it. The effectiveness of U.S. strategy will be based on our capacity to think like a networked enemy, in anticipation of how they may act in a variety of situations, aided by different resources. This goal requires that the American national security structure in turn organize itself for maximum efficiency, information sharing, and the ability to function quickly and effectively under new operational definitions. With this thorough understanding in mind, we need to craft an approach that specifically takes into account the following key factors to effectively wage a GCOIN:

1. Separating the enemy from the populace that provides support and sustenance. This, in turn, entails three basic missions: (a) Denial of enemy sanctuary; (b) Elimination of enemy freedom of movement; and (c) Denial of enemy resources and support;

2. Identification and neutralization of the enemy;

3. Creation of a secure environment—progressing from local to regional to global;

4. Ongoing and effective neutralization of enemy propaganda through the planning and execution of a comprehensive and integrated information operations and holistic civil affairs campaign in harmony with the first four tasks; and

5. Interagency efforts to build effective and responsible civil governance mechanisms that eliminate the fundamental causes of terrorism and insurgency.

In conclusion, al-Qaeda may be compared to the archetypal shark in the water that must keep moving forward—no matter how slowly or incrementally—or die. In al-Qaeda's context, this means adapting and adjusting to our countermeasures while simultaneously searching to identify new targets and vulnerabilities. In this respect, al-Qaeda's capacity to continue to prosecute this struggle is a direct reflection of both the movement's resiliency and the continued resonance of its ideology. Accordingly, if the threat we face is constantly changing and evolving, so must our policies and responses be regularly reviewed, updated, and adjusted. In this struggle, we cannot afford to rest on past laurels or be content with security that may have proven effective yesterday and today, but could likely prove inadequate tomorrow given this process of terrorist change and evolution.

Al-Qaeda's "operational durability" thus has enormous significance for U.S. counterterrorism strategy and policy. Because it has this malleable resiliency, it cannot be destroyed or defeated in a single tactical, military engagement or series of engagements—much less ones exclusively dependent on the application of conventional forces and firepower. To a significant degree, our ability to carry out such missions effectively will depend on the ability of American strategy to adjust and adapt to changes we see in the nature and character of our adversaries.

The CHAIRMAN. Thank you very much, Dr. Hoffman, for that remarkable paper and the insights you have presented to our hearing.

We call now on Mr. Andrew Kohut for his testimony.

STATEMENT OF MR. ANDREW KOHUT, PRESIDENT, PEW RESEARCH CENTER, WASHINGTON, DC

Mr. KOHUT. Thank you for the opportunity to help the committee understand the attitudes of people in the Muslim world, toward the West, toward the United States, toward the issues related to the war on terrorism.

Since 2002, the Pew Global Attitudes Project which I direct has interviewed more than 110,000 people in 50 countries, many of them Arab countries or predominantly Muslim countries in Africa and in Asia. I would like to do two things today: To update you on views toward the United States and the attitudes toward terrorism in the Muslim countries, but also tell you about a new survey that we conducted this year which was a broader investigation about how people in the Muslim world and Westerners view each other on a personal and individual level, and I think it has great bearing on the work of this committee.

First, the Global Attitudes Project has more generally documented the rise of anti-Americanism around the world since its inception in 2002. We have seen this to be especially the case in Muslim countries. Our most recent polls have found that the American people and the United States are viewed unfavorably in virtually all of the Muslim countries in which we have conducted surveys.

This is even the case in countries that are closely allied with the United States. For example, in Turkey just 12 percent of the people that we interviewed have a favorable view of the United States. Back in 2000 that was as high as 52 percent. Similarly, in Jordan 15 percent hold a positive view of the United States; in Pakistan, 27 percent hold a positive view of the United States.

The numbers are not very good anywhere. Of all of the countries that we have interviewed in 2 years that are predominantly Muslim, only in Morocco have we seen close to a majority saying anything positive about the United States. And, unlike in much of the rest of the world, the complaints aren't restricted just to the government, to the country at large, but also to the American people, who are held in low regard in the Muslim world.

Anti-Americanism in the Muslim world is driven by the United States' policies: the war in Iraq, most recently; the war on terrorism, generally; United States' support for Israel, probably most fully; and the general perception that the United States conducts its foreign policy unilaterally.

I'd like to just give you a quick overview of the important trends that we've seen in the past 5 years. First of all, anti-Americanism existed before the war in Iraq, in the Mideast and in Central Asia, but with the war in Iraq it really intensified. But the biggest impact is that with the war in Iraq, anti-Americanism became a global phenomenon in the Muslim world. We saw anti-Americanism, dislike of the country and the people, grow tremendously in Africa and in Asia where previously that had not been the case, notably in Indonesia, notably in Nigeria.

Second, the war on terrorism, while viewed with increasing suspicion among our European allies, has never been accepted in the Muslim world. It's seen as the United States picking on Muslim countries, as protecting Israel, and attempting to control the world.

Third, there has been substantial support for terrorism and terrorists among Muslim publics. Sizeable minorities in many Muslim countries have said that suicide bombings that target civilians in defense of Islam are sometimes or often justifiable, and significant numbers of people in many of these countries have expressed admiration and a positive view of Osama bin Laden.

While these trends have been mostly negative, we have seen some positive signs, too. The image of the United States improved markedly in Indonesia and somewhat even in Pakistan in response to the aid that we gave to victims of natural disasters in those countries.

We have seen support for terrorism decline somewhat in a number of countries, especially those who have had their own experience with it, in Morocco, Indonesia, Pakistan, and most recently in Jordan. Support for suicide bombing or believing that suicide bombing is justifiable decreased in the aftermath of attacks in those countries.

But while there is less support for suicide bombing and a less favorable regard for bin Laden, support for terrorism has far from disappeared in the Muslim world. In the survey that we conducted this year, 28, 29 percent of Jordanians and Egyptians see suicide bombing that targets civilians as justifiable.

Finally, our polling has found Muslims consistently saying that Western-style democracy can work in their countries, and that's a good thing. And despite the fact that they can't say, it's very difficult for them to say good things about the United States, they do tell us that they think that the United States supports democracy in their country.

These are among the broad, general trends that we have found in the Muslim world and in the Mideast, specifically. Now I want to turn to what we have learned in our most recent survey about how Muslim publics and Western publics view each other. That was the focus of our research in the current polling.

In the Muslim world, we did surveys in Indonesia, Pakistan, Jordan, Egypt, Turkey, and also in Nigeria, the Muslim part of Nigeria, which is about 50 percent of that country. In the West, we polled the United States, Britain, France, Germany, and Spain, but we also made a special effort to interview the Muslim minorities in the four European countries: Britain, France, Germany, and Spain.

Our overall conclusion in this survey was that a real divide does exist between the people of both cultures. The one thing that the Muslims and the Western respondents agreed on is that relations aren't good. That was the view of 70 percent of Germans, 55 percent of Americans, but it was matched by 64 percent of Turks and 58 percent of Egyptians who agree that the West and the Muslim people are not getting along very well.

When we probed the image of each people among the other, we saw very negative stereotyping. Westerners see Muslims as fanatical, violent, and not tolerant. Muslims see Westerners as selfish, immoral, greedy, as well as violent and fanatical. There's a lot of finger-pointing clearly going on in the way Westerners and Muslims look at each other.

And last year's controversy over the cartoons of Mohammed in Europe really highlighted it. Muslims saw Western disrespect for the Islamic religion. Westerners saw the Muslims as intolerant and not respecting freedom of expression. There are also very competing views about women. Each culture says the other side is not respectful of the way women are treated in their world.

Our second conclusion is that many Muslim publics have an aggrieved view of the West. Many blame U.S. and Western policies for the lack of prosperity in the Muslim world. Muslims feel more embittered toward the West and its people than vice versa. Muslim publics attribute more negative qualities to Western people than Westerners do to Muslims. They also rate Christians and especially Jews far less favorably than Europeans and Americans evaluate Muslim people.

Most Muslims—one of the most shocking findings of this survey, at least to me, was that most Muslims remain unconvinced that a group of Arab men carried out the 9/11 attacks. In Indonesia, 65 percent said, "No, it didn't happen that way." In Jordan, 53 percent said it didn't happen that way. Even in Turkey, 59 percent said it didn't happen that way. This is the same question that the Gallup organization had asked in about January or February of 2002, right after the attacks, and basically we found the same answers that Gallup found: Most Muslim publics in denial about who carried out these attacks.

On the other hand, while there is this aggrieved view in the Muslim world, Westerners are skeptical of Muslim values. Westerners, more often than Muslims, see a conflict between Islam and modernity. Westerners are less optimistic about the prospects for democracy in the Muslim world than are Muslims themselves, who, as I said earlier, have consistently told us that they believe Western-style democracy will work there.

This may reflect, the views of Westerners may reflect that Americans and Western Europeans are very dismayed about the Hamas election victory in Palestine, but certainly Muslim publics are not. They see it as good for the Palestinian people. They see it as good for the resolution of the conflict with Israel. Westerners also see more support for al-Qaeda in the Muslim world than do Muslims.

This poll has a lot of negative findings. We did find some positive things. First of all, there is not—following a bad year of riots and the 7/7 bombings, we didn't see an outright spike in hostility between Muslims and Westerners. The attitudes that I'm speaking about are of a more long-lasting, enduring nature. Majorities in France, Britain, and the United States retain generally favorable views of Muslims.

And, as I said earlier, there has been another decline in support for suicide bombing in a number of countries, but there still remains considerable support. Sizeable majorities in major Muslim countries say suicide bombing can be justified. Even among Europe's moderate Muslims, which I'll tell you a little bit more about, one in seven feels suicide bombings that target civilians can be justified under certain circumstances in defense of Islam.

I have to tell you, though, that the most troubling numbers are the ones that we got out of Nigeria. In Nigeria, 61 percent of the people that we interviewed, the Muslims that we interviewed, said they had a favorable view of Osama bin Laden, and 56 percent say most of the people that they know support radical groups like al-Qaeda.

We haven't gone back into Africa in any great detail since 2002. I did note the change in opinion. When we do go back, we can only hope that what we found in Nigeria isn't echoed among other Muslim publics.

With regard to the European Muslims, they hold a more temperate view of the West than do Muslims in the Mideast and Asia and Africa. European Muslims have more positive views of Westerners than those in the countries back home. They are less likely than other Europeans to see a conflict between modernity and Islam. They think it can work.

Most European Muslims expressed favorable opinions of Christians, and more favorable opinions of Jews than do Muslims in other countries. In France, in particular, there are relatively positive views among French Muslims of Jews.

Muslims in Europe do worry about their future, but their concern is more economic than religious or cultural. Generally, European Muslims show signs of favoring a moderate version of Islam.

One of the things I would like to emphasize, if you look at our study carefully, there is no clear European point of view about Muslims. There is not a clear European Muslim point of view. The views of French, German, Spanish, and British Muslims are quite distinct.

British Muslims are the most anxious about their future, they're the most concerned about extremism, but they have the largest minority expressing very antagonistic views toward Westerners. French Muslims are the most integrated, eager to be part of the French society, and most welcomed by the general public. German Muslims are the most likely to consider Europeans hostile, and the German public is least accepting of Muslim immigrants of the four publics that we've questioned.

I would like to conclude that it's no secret that the United States has an image problem in the Muslim world. Iraq has intensified it and broadened discontent with America and its people among Muslims in the Mideast, Africa, and Asia. There is little sign in our surveys that this has meaningfully changed over the past 3 years.

In some predominantly Muslim countries, things have gotten better. In other countries, things have gotten a little worse. But the bottom line remains the same: We are poorly regarded by most

Muslim people, and significant numbers of them express at least tacit support for terrorist tactics and the enemies of the United States, although the trends have been going in the right direction on these measures.

As the events of the past year in Europe have indicated, there is a broad divide between Westerners and Muslims around the world. Misunderstanding, value differences, economic-based resentment have led to suspicion and a mutually acknowledged divide or clash of civilizations.

The good news is that Muslims in Europe are nonetheless far more moderate and positive toward the West than Muslims living in the Mideast, Africa, and Asia. Their attitudes and the attitudes of the general population in the host countries suggest that exposure might indeed lead to improved understanding, mostly. Thank you very much.

[The prepared statement of Mr. Kohut follows:]

PREPARED STATEMENT OF ANDREW KOHUT, PRESIDENT, PEW RESEARCH CENTER, WASHINGTON, DC

Thank you for the opportunity to help the committee better understand the attitudes of people in the Muslim world toward the West, the United States in particular, and issues related to the war on terrorism.

Since its first public opinion survey in 2002, the Pew Global Attitudes project has conducted seven surveys totaling 110,000 interviews in 50 nations, including many Arab and majority Muslim countries.[1] I would like to do two things today: First, give you an update on the image of the United States and attitudes toward terrorism in Muslim countries and, second, tell you about the results of a broader investigation that we made in this year's survey regarding how Muslims and Westerners regard each other.

FAVORABLE OPINION OF THE UNITED STATES

[Amounts in percent]

	1999/ 2000	2002	2003	2004	2005	2006
Egypt	—	—	—	—	—	30
Jordan	—	25	1	5	21	15
Morocco	77	—	27	27	49	—
Lebanon*	—	30	15	—	22	—
Turkey	52	30	15	30	23	12
Pakistan	23	10	13	21	23	27
Indonesia	—	61	15	—	38	30
Nigeria*	—	72	38	—	—	32

*Muslims only.

1999/2000 trends from Office of Research, U.S. Dept. of State.

First, since their inception, our surveys have documented the rise of anti-Americanism around the world, but especially in predominately Muslim countries. In our most recent polls, the United States and the American people are regarded unfavorably by sizable majorities among seven of eight Muslim publics surveyed.

DISLIKE OF AMERICANS TOO—2005/2006

[Amounts in percent]

	Favorable	Unfavorable	DK
Egypt	36	63	1=100
Jordan	38	61	1=100
Morocco	62	30	7=99

---

[1] Full details of the surveys in this program can be found at www.pewglobal.org.

DISLIKE OF AMERICANS TOO—2005/2006—Continued

[Amounts in percent]

	Favorable	Unfavorable	DK
Lebanon*	22	47	1=100
Turkey	17	69	14=100
Pakistan	27	52	20=99
Indonesia	36	60	5=101
Nigeria*	23	75	3=101

*Muslims only.

Figures for Morocco and Lebanon are from 2005.

Most troubling is the extent of anti-Americanism in countries that are important allies of the United States. In Turkey, just 12 percent hold a positive opinion of the United States, down from as high as 52 percent in 2000. Similarly, only 15 percent in Jordan and 27 percent in Pakistan rate the United States positively. Views of the American people are only somewhat more favorable than opinions of the United States generally in the Mideast and among Muslims in Asia and Africa.

SUPPORT FOR SUICIDE BOMBING*

[Amounts in percent]

	Violence against civilian targets justified			
	Often/Sometimes	Rarely	Never	DK
Jordan	29	28	43	*=100
Spring 2005	57	31	11	1=100
Summer 2002	43	22	26	8=99
Egypt	28	25	45	3=101
Turkey	17	9	61	14=101
Spring 2005	14	6	66	13=99
March 2004	15	9	67	9=100
Summer 2002	13	7	64	14=98
Pakistan	14	8	69	8=99
Spring 2005	25	19	46	10=100
March 2004	41	8	35	16=100
Summer 2002	33	5	38	23=99
Indonesia	10	18	71	1=100
Spring 2005	15	18	66	1=100
Summer 2002	27	16	54	3=100
Nigeria	46	23	28	3=100

* Asked of Muslims only.

Anti-Americanism is largely driven by aversion to United States policies, such as the war in Iraq, the war on terrorism, and United States support for Israel, in addition to the general perception that the United States fails to consider the interests of other countries when it acts in the international arena. Here are some important trends that we have seen over the past 5 years:

- Anti-Americanism worsened in the Mideast in response to the war in Iraq—but it soared among Muslims in other parts of the world that previously did not view the United States poorly—notably in Indonesia and Nigeria.
- The war on terrorism, while viewed with increasing suspicion among our European allies, has never been accepted as legitimate by Muslims. It has been seen as the United States picking on Muslim countries, protecting Israel, and attempting to control the world.
- There has been substantial support for terrorism and terrorists among Muslim publics. Sizable minorities in many Muslim countries have said that suicide bombings that target civilians can often or sometimes be justified in defense of Islam and appreciable numbers have expressed support for Osama bin Laden.

But while the trends have been mostly negative, we have seen some positive signs too:

- The image of the United States improved markedly in Indonesia in 2004 and slightly in Pakistan in 2005 in response to United States aid to victims of natural disasters in these countries.

- Support for terrorism has declined somewhat in a number of countries, especially those that have had their own experience with it. We have seen this in Morocco, Indonesia, Pakistan, and, most recently and dramatically, Jordan, following last year's attack in Amman.

It is important to note, however, that while we see less support for suicide bombing and less favorable regard for bin Laden, support for terrorism has far from disappeared in the Muslim world.

- Finally, our polling has found Muslims consistently saying that Western-style democracy can work in their countries and, despite their dislike of the United States, many believe that the United States supports increased democracy in their countries.

These are among the most important findings among Muslims in our recent surveys, specifically about the United States and American policies. Our polling this year looked at a broader question that is pertinent to the work of this committee—how do Western and Muslim publics view each other?

In the Muslim world we polled in Indonesia, Pakistan, Jordan, Egypt, and Turkey. In the West, the survey included the United States, Great Britain, France, Germany, and Spain. We interviewed the Muslim minorities in the four European countries, as well, to get some insight into the views of this rapidly growing segment of the population.

Our overall conclusion is that a real divide exists between Western and Muslim people, reflected by a year marked by riots over cartoon portrayals of Muhammad, a major terrorist attack in London, and continuing wars in Iraq and Afghanistan.

The rare point of consensus in the survey was that both Muslims and Westerners are convinced that relations between the peoples are generally bad. In the West, 70 percent of Germans and 55 percent of Americans think so. This is matched by 64 percent of Turks and 58 percent of Egyptians who believe this, too. Large majorities of Muslims blame Westerners for the problem. Many Europeans and Americans point their fingers at the Muslims, but many in the West also accept some responsibility for the problem.

ARE MUSLIMS RESPECTFUL OF WOMEN?

[Amounts in percent]

	Yes*	No
Non-Muslims in:		
Great Britain	26	59
France	23	77
United States	19	69
Germany	17	80
Spain	12	83

*Percentage who associate characteristic with Muslims/people in Western countries.

ARE WESTERNERS RESPECTFUL OF WOMEN?

[Amounts in percent]

	Yes*	No
Muslims in:		
Spain	82	13
France	77	23
Germany	73	22
Great Britain	49	44
Turkey	42	39
Egypt	40	52
Indonesia	38	50
Jordan	38	53
Pakistan	22	52

*Percentage who associate characteristic with Muslims/people in Western countries.

Each side has a mostly negative image of the other people. Westerners see Muslims as fanatical, violent, and not tolerant. Muslims see Westerners as selfish, immoral, and greedy, as well as violent and fanatical.

Last year's controversy over cartoons of Muhammad highlights the divide between Muslims and the West. Most people in Jordan, Egypt, Indonesia, and Turkey blame the controversy on Western nations' disrespect for the Islamic religion. In contrast, majorities of Americans and Western Europeans who have heard of the controversy say Muslims' intolerance to different points of view is more to blame.

The chasm between Muslims and the West is also seen in judgments about how the other civilization treats women. Western publics, by lopsided margins, do not think of Muslims as "respectful of women." But half or more in four of the five Muslim publics surveyed say the same thing about people in the West.

A second conclusion of the poll is that Muslims have an aggrieved view of the West. Many blame United States and Western policies for their lack of prosperity. For example, this is the opinion of 66 percent of Jordanians and 59 percent of Egyptians who think that their country should be more prosperous than it is. Westerners most often point to government corruption and Muslim fundamentalism as the cause of the problem.

DID ARABS CARRY OUT 9/11 ATTACKS?*

[Amounts in percent]

	Yes	No
British Muslims	17	56
French Muslims	48	46
German Muslims	35	44
Spanish Muslims	33	35
Indonesia	16	65
Egypt	32	59
Turkey	16	59
Jordan	39	53
Pakistan	15	41
Nigerian Muslims	42	47

*Asked of Muslims only.

A number of measures in these surveys show Muslims feeling more embittered toward the West and its people than vice versa. They attribute more negative qualities to Western people than Westerners do to Muslims. They also rate Christians and Jews less favorably than Europeans and Americans rate Muslims. One of the startling findings of the survey is that most Muslims remain unconvinced that Arabs carried out the September 11 attacks. In Indonesia, 65 percent, in Jordan 53 percent, and in Turkey 59 percent deny that the attacks were carried out by Arab men.

While Muslims feel aggrieved, Westerners are skeptical and wary of Muslim values. For example, Western Europeans and Americans see a conflict between Islam and modernity more often than do Muslims themselves. Westerners also see somewhat more support for al-Qaeda in the Muslim world than do Muslims. The current poll finds Europeans are less optimistic about prospects for democracy in Muslim countries than Muslims are. This may reflect our finding that Americans and Western Europeans are dismayed over the Hamas election victory. Muslims in the Mideast, Asia, and Africa see this as a positive development for the Palestinian people.

In this regard, this year's poll also finds increasing sympathy for Israel in Western Europe. Europeans do not match American public opinion—where the percentage sympathetic to Israelis is more than three times greater than that sympathetic to Palestinians—but it is moving in that direction.

The good news in this poll is that even after a bad year, there was not a spike in outright hostility toward Muslims among Westerners or vice versa. These negative perceptions are of a more long-standing nature. And, as noted above, this poll shows a decline in support for terrorism in important Muslim countries. However, having said that, sizable minorities in major Muslim countries say suicide bombing can be justified. Even among Europe's Muslims, one-in-seven feel suicide bombings against civilian targets can be justified.

Osama bin Laden is viewed positively by one-in-three in Pakistan and Indonesia and one-in-four in Egypt and Jordan. The most troublesome numbers are out of Nigeria, where 61 percent of Muslims in that religiously divided country express confidence in bin Laden. Muslims there are highly critical of Westerners and no fewer than 56 percent say that most or many of their countrymen support extremist groups like al-Qaeda—by far the highest in the poll.

In sharp contrast, the survey found that European Muslims hold more temperate views of the West than do Muslims in the Mideast, Africa, and Asia. Muslims in

Great Britain, France, Germany, and Spain have more positive views of Westerners than do Muslims in the Mideast and Asia. They largely hold positive views toward Christians and have less negative views of Jews than do Muslims in the Mideast and Asia. This is especially true in France.

The survey did find that Muslims in Europe worry about their future, but their concern is more economic than religious or cultural. And while there are some signs of tension between Europe's majority populations and its Muslim minorities, Muslims there do not generally believe that most Europeans are hostile toward people of their faith.

MUSLIMS MORE CONCERNED ABOUT UNEMPLOYMENT THAN RELIGIOUS AND CULTURAL ISSUES

[Amounts in percent]

	Muslims in			
	Great Britain	France	Germany	Spain
Very worried about:				
Unemployment	46	52	56	55
Islamic extremism	44	30	23	22
Decline of religion	45	21	18	18
Influence of pop culture	44	17	18	17
Modern roles for women	22	16	9	10

Despite some tension, there is little evidence of a widespread backlash against Muslim immigrants among the general publics in Great Britain, France, Germany, and Spain. Majorities continue to express concerns about rising Islamic identity and extremism, but those worries have not intensified in most of the countries surveyed over the past 12 turbulent months. Still, over a third of Muslims in France and one-in-four in Spain say they have had a bad experience as a result of their religion or ethnicity.

EXPERIENCES OF MUSLIMS IN EUROPE

[Amounts in percent]

	Europeans hostile to Muslims?	Had a bad personal experience?
	Yes*	Yes
Muslims in:		
Germany	51	19
Great Britain	42	28
France	39	37
Spain	31	25

*Percent saying most or many Europeans are hostile toward Muslims.

Opinions held by Muslims in Europe—as well as opinions about Muslims among Europe's majority populations—vary significantly by country. No clear European point of view emerges with regard to the Muslim experience, either among Muslims or in the majority populations, on many issues. British Muslims are the most anxious about their future and most concerned about extremism.

French Muslims are the most integrated and are less likely than others to primarily identify as Muslims and more often see themselves as French first. They are more likely to say they want to adopt European customs than are Muslims in other European countries. German Muslims are the most likely to consider Europeans hostile, although many fewer report a bad personal experience.

Generally, European Muslims show signs of favoring a moderate version of Islam. With the exception of Spanish Muslims, they tend to see a struggle being waged between moderates and Islamic fundamentalists. Among those who see an ongoing conflict, substantial majorities in all four countries say they generally side with the moderates.

MOST SEEING STRUGGLE SIDE WITH MODERATES

[Amounts in percent]

	See a struggle*	And identify with—	
		Moderates	Fundamental-ists
Muslims in:			
Great Britain	58	38	15
France	56	50	6
Germany	49	36	7
Spain	21	14	4
Nigeria	36	18	17

*Think there is a struggle in (survey country) between moderate Muslims and Islamic fundamentalists.

Most French and British Muslims think women are better off in their countries than in most Muslim countries. About half of German and Spanish Muslims agree, and very few think women actually have it better in most Muslim countries. Moreover, most are not concerned about Muslim women in Europe taking on modern roles in society (although substantial minorities worry about this).

Muslims in Europe are most sharply distinguished from the majority populations on opinions about external issues—America, the war on terrorism, Iran, and the Middle East. European Muslims give the United States lower favorability ratings than do general publics in Europe and, in particular, they give the American people lower ratings. The war on terror is extremely unpopular among minority Muslim populations.

CONTRASTING OPINIONS IN EUROPE OF AMERICANS

[Amounts in percent]

	Favorable opinion
Among general population in:	
Great Britain	69
Germany	66
France	65
Spain	37
Among Muslims in:	
Great Britain	39
Germany	44
France	48
Spain	33

To conclude, it is no secret that the United States has an image problem in the Muslim world. The war in Iraq intensified and broadened discontent with America and its people among Muslims in the Mideast, Africa, and Asia. There is little sign from our surveys that this has meaningfully changed over the past 3 years. In some predominately Muslim countries there has been improvement, while in others a worsening of attitudes.

But the bottom line remains the same. We are poorly regarded by most Muslims and significant numbers of them express at least tacit support for terrorist tactics and enemies of the United States, such as Osama bin Laden.

As events of the past year in Europe have indicated, there is a broad divide between Westerners and Muslims around the world. Our latest surveys have detailed the nature of the complaints from both sides. Misunderstanding, value differences, and economics-based resentment have led to suspicion and created a mutually acknowledged divide. The good news is that Muslims in Europe, despite their concerns about their future are nonetheless far more moderate and positive toward the West than are Muslims living in the Mideast, Africa, and Asia. Their attitudes and the general populations in the host countries suggest that exposure may lead to improved understanding, mostly.

The CHAIRMAN. Thank you very much, Mr. Kohut.

We would like to hear now from Mr. Ahmed, if you would proceed.

STATEMENT OF AMBASSADOR AKBAR S. AHMED, IBN KHALDUN CHAIR OF ISLAMIC STUDIES, SCHOOL OF INTERNATIONAL SERVICE, AMERICAN UNIVERSITY, WASHINGTON, DC

Ambassador AHMED. Thank you, sir. A great honor to be speaking to this committee. I am especially thankful to Chairman Lugar for inviting me.

I have been arguing since 9/11 that terrorism, the war on terror, cannot be understood without looking at the big picture, and this is what I'll do this morning. Terrorism is one small piece of the jigsaw puzzle, and that has been the limitation of the strategy thus far.

Let us remind ourselves why relations between the United States and Muslim world are so important. Islam is a world civilization of 1.4 billion people and growing, 57 states, one of which is nuclear for the time being, and there are some 7 million Muslims living in the United States. Besides, the United States has troops fighting and losing lives in two Muslim nations, Iraq and Afghanistan.

Neither the war on terror nor a serious tackling of the global crises facing all of us on this planet, crises like global warming, poverty, the population explosion, the religious and ethnic conflicts, none of these can be resolved unless the vast and highly significant world of Islam is brought into a mutually respectful partnership with the rest of the world, especially with the United States, the sole superpower and leader of the world.

As a Muslim scholar living in Washington, DC, I felt on 9/11 that I had to do whatever little I could to create understanding between the two. I also knew that my extensive field experiences in charge of some of the most inaccessible areas of the Muslim world, such as South Waziristan Agency where Osama bin Laden is supposed to be hiding, would be an added advantage.

This urge took me on travels in the Muslim world, to nine countries in the three major regions of the Muslim world—the Middle East, South Asia, and Far East Asia—from February to April 2006. I was accompanied by a small but enthusiastic group of American research assistants.

We were able to discuss these issues with a whole range of people, from President Musharraf to prime ministers, princes, sheikhs, professors, students, taxi drivers, the whole gamut of society. We visited mosques, madrassas, university campuses, and classrooms. And the project was sponsored by three leading institutions in Washington: American University, the Brookings Institution, and the Pew Forum.

Now, at the conclusion of the trip, my team and I felt that there was bad news and there was good news, so the bad news first. Throughout the travels we encountered very high levels of anti-Americanism and anti-Semitism. I have never encountered such intensity of emotion.

The Muslim world, in the years of the cold war when the United States was so obviously the moral power, admired and respected the United States. Today we found that many Muslims do not see the United States as the moral power it once used to be. In fact, many of the people we surveyed throughout the nine countries said that they would prefer Saddam Hussein, the most ruthless and vile of dictators, to the Americans in Iraq.

In Turkey, the most popular film ever made is called "Valley of the Wolves: Iraq." It's in theaters everywhere, and it is a crudely anti-American film which shows a group of "Rambo" Turkish soldiers fighting against the evil United States soldiers.

Even in the moderate country of Indonesia—and I have bad news for my colleague who referred to Nigeria in hope that Osama bin Laden would only be restricted as a role model there—on university campuses we found that bin Laden was the number one role model. He is now referred to as "Sheikh" Osama bin Laden. That is bad news. Perhaps you don't understand the nuance, but for a Muslim like me it is bad news. Anyone trying to preach and promote moderation will find this a major hurdle, because "Sheikh" means he has been elevated to a religious status.

The Muslim world focuses on action rather than rhetoric, and right now they are seeing cold-blooded rapes in Iraq by United States soldiers, the encouragement of torture, and they feel they are not seeing the ideals of the United States, of democracy, human rights, and acceptance of diversity, that it once so proudly and clearly stood for. One affluent woman who used to live in the United States even told my team that she was scared to bring her grandchildren back to the United States because of the way they treat Muslims. That is the bad news.

Furthermore, there is a widespread perception in the Muslim world that Islam is under attack from the United States. As we saw with the Danish cartoon controversy and the desecration of the Quran story, Muslims all over the world are very passionate about their religion and their Prophet. It is a culture with high reverence for and sensitivity to these religious symbols and traditions.

Now let me explain what's going on in the Muslim world. There is a common belief here in the West that all this begins on 9/11. In fact, the story goes back almost two centuries. There has been a struggle within Islam, not so much for the soul of Islam but for the politics and the culture of Islam, between three broad interpretations of Islam: Between an orthodox, literalist interpretation, between one that advocates synthesis and receptivity to the West, and third the universalist or mystic response to the world. Three defined but distinct responses. So some of the labels that we are seeing after 9/11 cause nothing but confusing, and if you get your labeling wrong, you're going to run into problems later on because all your strategy is going to be wrong.

Right now the warfare in Iraq and Afghanistan, the perceived attacks on Islam, and the insensitivity to culture are all reinforcing the strong orthodox, literalist interpretation of Islam, and this is now spreading throughout the Muslim world. So remember the formula: The more you push the Muslim world, the greater the support for the literalist, orthodox, the more you marginalize the moderates, the more you wipe out the mystics and the humanists. This is the simple formula we need to appreciate.

There is cause and effect here. I refer to anti-Americanism and anti-Semitism but would like to introduce another word, related, perhaps not directly, but related to the concept of hatred, which is Islamophobia, the hatred of all things Islamic, although these concepts are different, but Islamophobia after 9/11 has gained momentum.

The reasons are obvious. The 19 hijackers on 9/11 were all Muslim. Some of the most wanted people on the planet, Osama bin Laden and so on, are Muslim. So people generally and too easily equate Muslims to terrorists and extremists.

The result of this Islamophobia has been attacks on Islam and on Muslims. Muslims then find there is little hope of getting justice in this climate, and are sometimes pushed toward acts of violence. I do not wish to condone these acts by any means, and have condemned them, but I want to put the discussion in some context.

Now for the good news. This ignorance and hatred can be challenged and can change. Just as Muslims are sensitive to attacks on Islam, Muslims are also very receptive to the positive messages from within Islam. I encourage, Chairman Lugar, you and your colleagues, and indeed the American people, to learn about Islam and find the common bonds between the two civilizations.

Indeed, American values of equality, justice, knowledge, and compassion, as seen in the respect for human rights, are shared explicitly with Islam. Remind the leaders in the Muslim world and the people there of these common values, without giving lectures to them. Remind them of the context.

Remind them that beheadings, suicide bombings, are not part of Islam, and that two of the greatest attributes of God in Islam are the "merciful" and the "compassionate." These two words are repeated by Muslims throughout the day all over the planet. Speaking about the common values shared by the Founding Fathers of the United States and the ideals of Islam will make a powerful and long-lasting impact on the hearts and minds of Muslims.

Furthermore, Muslims, Christians, and Jews share deep bonds between them. Muslims are asked in the Quran to recognize the Jews and the Christians as "people of the book," and they hold a special place in our theology. A common figure who inspires us and who we share as a common patriarch and ancestor is Abraham. And as for the love of Jesus in Islam, I urge you to read the "Jesus poems" of Rumi, who is such a popular poet in the United States. We share the notion of an omnipotent, universal God, the Ten Commandments, many of the central values. While political and historical events have divided the two, examples of peaceful coexistence also exist.

So during these travels in the Muslim world, I would use these ideas, and I believe that the first, most important step was to talk about dialog, understanding, and friendship. So dialog, No. 1, understanding, No. 2, friendship, No. 3. You cannot have simple dialog and leave it there.

One of the ways I would deal with the anti-Americanism and anti-Semitism was to talk of the dialogs I am having and the friendships that have been created here in Washington, DC. I mentioned my friends like Jean and Steve Case, Ambassador Doug and Ann Holladay, Bishop John and Karen Chane, Senior Rabbi Bruce Lustig and his wife Amy, and Dr. Lachland Reed, and many other friends like this. In my travels I mentioned these wonderful Americans who became my friends and who reached out to me after 9/11, seeing a lonely stranger in their midst.

I mentioned how I am personally inspired by the example of my friend, Judea Pearl, who lost his only son, Danny Pearl, in a brutal, savage, and senseless killing in Karachi. Having gotten to know Judea as a friend over the years because of our dialogs conducted nationally and internationally in promoting Jewish-Muslim understanding, I have seen the heroic transformation of a personal tragedy into building a bridge to reach out and understand the very civilization that produced the killers who took his son's life. I would point out that these friendships have also helped to transform the relationship between Muslims, Jews, and Christians in the United States.

And please keep the context in mind. I was quoting these names in a mosque in Damascus, where I was asked to deliver the post-sermon talk on a Friday, very significant for Muslims; in madrassas in Deoband and Delhi, in speeches in Islamabad, at the Royal Institute in Amman.

I would finally ask my team of young Americans to speak, and I would introduce them as the best ambassadors we have between the United States and the Muslim world, as intrepid Americans who represented the best ideals of America. And for commentary on our travels, please see Beliefnet.com for articles by Dilshad Ali and the young Americans who accompanied me, Hailey Woldt and Jonathan Hayden. And I am grateful, Chairman Lugar, for giving permission to bring them here. They are here with me this morning.

As a professor on campus I would also recommend some books, and this is what I would urge for you to do. This is an instinct, I suspect a genetic instinct in all professors. We can't restrain from doing this.

My first book is by my friend, Dr. Jonathan Sacks, the Chief Rabbi of the United Kingdom, and it is called "The Dignity of Difference." It is a powerful plea for Abrahamic understanding in the age of globalization.

The second book I would recommend to my Muslim audiences and to my American audience this morning is also by a friend, Karen Armstrong, and her book is "The Battle for God." In this book Karen illustrates how the three different faiths, Judaism, Christianity, and Islam, are all going through a period of intense internal debate in what she calls the "fundamentalist" mode.

And, third, to keep a balance—you've got a Jewish, a Christian, a Muslim author—I would recommend my own book, "Islam Under Siege," which argues that we are living in a world in which societies are feeling under siege, whether American societies, Israeli societies, or Muslim societies. And when societies feel under siege, they tend to be defensive and there is limited scope for wisdom or compassion.

Essentially, this boils down to one recommendation, and perhaps you may dismiss it as too idealistic, but that is the only way to make lasting peace for the United States and the Muslim world. It is to create bonds of friendship across religion, race, and tradition. I have discovered in a very personal sense, not only as a scholar on campus but as someone involved in a very realistic, pragmatic way in dealing with real life situations, that once friendship develops, everything can change. Without these friendships, dialog itself remains a restricted exchange of ideas and leads to little else.

This suggestion may be unlikely, particularly with the growing situation in the Middle East, but without genuine friendships we cannot expect any major changes in how we are dealing with the political situations on the ground. Take the example of the Palestinians and the Israelis. Too often the two view each other as enemies and are not prepared to concede anything except in terms of an advantage to themselves.

The result is that even if there are concessions, they are seen to be a result of bitter negotiations which continue to leave acrimony on both sides. But if both parties are able to create friendships and then meet as friends, the situation will be very different, and the peace process itself may take a new momentum and a new meaning.

In conclusion, this is a great leap of imagination I am asking you to make, but the exercise to understand the Muslim world is not a luxury for the United States. It is an absolute imperative. It is the first step, allowing you to confront the looming series of world crises which we face in the 21st century. And as you on the panel are those who this great Nation looks to for wisdom and guidance, I plead with you this morning to set aside the partisan and parochial issues and focus on the challenges of providing justice, compassion, and friendship in this dangerous, uncertain, and violent time.

Thank you.

[The prepared statement of Ambassador Ahmed follows:]

PREPARED STATEMENT OF AMBASSADOR AKBAR S. AHMED, IBN KHALDUN CHAIR OF ISLAMIC STUDIES, SCHOOL OF INTERNATIONAL SERVICE, AMERICAN UNIVERSITY, WASHINGTON, DC

On that catastrophic day of September 11, 2001, I was acutely aware that the sole superpower of the world, the United States, which had the capacity to show the way to solving the global challenges that faced us, could be diverted in an endless war of revenge and anger. This event set the United States directly in confrontation with the world of Islam as it launched its "war on terror." The complicated confrontation is bleeding the energies and resources of both civilizations. It is diverting the United States from its greater mission of showing the way to solve the problems that face the planet and concerns every human on earth. Whether the United States accepts the role as the moral leader for the 21st century willingly or not, the United States is the sole superpower and leader.

Let us remind ourselves why a dialog between the United States and the Muslim world is important. Islam is a world civilization of 1.4 billion people, 57 states—one of which is nuclear for the time-being—and there are 7 million Muslims living in the United States. Besides, the United States has troops fighting and losing lives in two Muslim nations—Iraq and Afghanistan. Neither the war on terror nor a serious tackling of the global crises facing us can be resolved unless the vast and highly significant world of Islam is brought into a mutually respectful partnership with the rest of the world—especially the United States.

As a Muslim scholar living in Washington, DC, I felt I had to do whatever little I could to create understanding between the two. I also knew that my extensive field experiences in charge of some of the most inaccessible areas of the Muslim world—such as South Waziristan Agency where Osama bin Laden is supposed to be hiding—would be an added advantage for both sides. This urge took me on travels in the Muslim world to nine countries in the three major regions of the Muslim world—the Middle East, South Asia, and Far East Asia, from February to April, 2006. I was accompanied by a small but enthusiastic group of American research assistants. We were able to discuss these issues with a whole range of people from President Musharraf to prime ministers, princes, sheikhs, professors, and students. We visited mosques, madrassahs, university campuses, and classrooms. The project was sponsored by three leading institutions in Washington DC—American University, the Brookings Institution, and the Pew Forum.

Throughout the travels we encountered very high levels of anti-Americanism and anti-Semitism. I have never encountered such intensity of emotion. The Muslim world, in the years of the cold war when the United States was so obviously the moral power, admired and respected the United States. Today, we found that many Muslims do not see the United States as the moral power it once used to be; in fact, many of the people we surveyed throughout the nine countries said that they would prefer Saddam Hussein, the most ruthless and vile of dictators, to the Americans in Iraq. In Turkey, the most popular film ever made called "Valley of the Wolves: Iraq" was in theaters when we were there. It is crudely anti-American and it shows a group of "Rambo" Turkish soldiers fighting against the "evil" United States soldiers. Even in the moderate country of Indonesia, the No. 1 role model for young Indonesians is Osama bin Laden—who is now widely called "Sheikh" as a mark of religious respect. The Muslim world focuses on action rather than rhetoric and right now they are seeing cold-blooded rapes in Iraq by United States soldiers, the encouragement of torture, and they feel they are not seeing the ideals of the United States of democracy, human rights, and acceptance of diversity that it once so proudly and clearly stood for. One affluent woman who used to live in the United States even told my team that she was "scared" to bring her grandchildren to the United States now because of the way they treat Muslims. That is the bad news.

Furthermore, there is a widespread perception in the Muslim world that Islam is under attack from the United States and the West. As we saw with the Danish cartoon controversy and the desecration of the Quran, Muslims all over the world are very passionate about their religion and their Prophet. It is a culture with high reverence for and sensitivity to these religious symbols and traditions.

There is a struggle within Islam which has been in play for centuries but is now erupting, between the more literalist interpreters of Islam and the more receptive and mystic forms. Right now, the warfare in Iraq and Afghanistan, perceived attacks on Islam, and insensitivity to culture are all reinforcing the strong, literalist interpretations of Islam. More outward signs of orthodoxy are spreading throughout the Muslim world, even to Indonesia. The greater the perception that Islam is under attack, then, the greater the support for those Muslims who stand up as champions of Islam. There is clearly cause and effect here.

I am referring to anti-Americanism and anti-Semitism but we need to keep in mind Islamophobia which means a hatred of Islam and prejudice against Muslims. Although they are different to each other, I suggest we need to understand their impact on each other. Islamophobia after 9/11 has gained momentum. The reason is obvious: The 19 hijackers on 9/11 were all Muslim. Some of the most wanted people in the world like Osama bin Laden are Muslim. People too readily equated all Muslims to terrorists and extremists. The result of this Islamophobia has been attacks on Islam and on Muslims. Muslims find that there is little hope of getting justice in this climate and are sometimes pushed toward acts of violence. I do not wish to condone these acts by any means and have condemned them, but I want to put the discussion in some context.

But there is good news. This ignorance and hatred can be challenged and can change. Just as Muslims are sensitive to "attacks" on Islam, Muslims are also very receptive to the positive messages from within Islam. I encourage all of the Senators and American people to learn about Islam and find the common bonds between the two civilizations.

Indeed, American values of equality, justice, knowledge, and compassion (as seen in the respect for human rights) are shared explicitly with Islam. Remind the leaders and the people there of these common values without giving a lecture—remind them of this especially in their own context as well. Beheadings and suicide bombings are not part of Islam—remind them of that and that two of the greatest attributes of God in Islam are the "merciful" and the "compassionate." Speaking about the common values shared by the Founding Fathers of the United States and the ideals of Islam will make a powerful and long-lasting impact on the hearts and minds of Muslims.

Furthermore, Muslims, Christians, and Jews share deep bonds between them. Muslims are asked in the Quran to recognize the Jews and the Christians as "people of the book" and they hold a special place in our theology. A common figure who inspires us and who we share as a common patriarch and ancestor is Abraham. As for the love of Jesus in Islam, I urge you to read the "Jesus Poems" of Rumi who is such a popular poet in the United States. The notions of an omnipotent, universal God, the Ten Commandments, many of the central values, are shared by the religions. Political and historical events have divided us, but examples of peaceful coexistence between the three religions can also be seen in history and contemporary society.

I also used this idea to encourage understanding during my travels. The first and most important steps were to encourage dialog, understanding, and friendship. One of the ways I would deal with the anti-Americanism and anti-Semitism was to talk of the dialogs I am having and the friendships that have been created between Jews, Christians, and Muslims and give my own personal example. I mentioned my friends like Jean and Steve Case, Doug and Ann Holladay, Bishop John and Karen Chane, Rabbi Bruce Lustig and his wife Amy, and Dr. Lachland Reed. In my travels and talks, I mentioned these wonderful Americans who became my friends and who reached out to me after 9/11 seeing a lonely stranger in their midst.

I mentioned how I am personally inspired by the example of my friend, Judea Pearl, who lost his only son, Danny Pearl, in a brutal, savage, and senseless killing in Karachi. Having gotten to know him as a friend over the years, because of our dialogs conducted nationally and internationally in promoting Jewish Muslim understanding, I have seen the heroic transformation of a personal tragedy into building a bridge to reach out and understand the very civilization that produced the killers who took his son's life. I would point out that these friendships have also helped to transform the relationship between Muslims, Jews, and Christians in the United States.

Please keep the context in mind: I was quoting these names in a mosque in Damascus where I was asked to deliver the post-sermon talk on a Friday, in madrassahs in Deoband and Delhi, and in speeches in Islamabad, as well as the Royal Institute in Amman.

I would finally ask my team of young Americans to speak and I would introduce them as the best ambassadors we have between the United States and the Muslim world as intrepid Americans who represented the best ideals of America (for commentary on our travels see Beliefnet.com for articles by Dilshad Ali, and the young Americans who accompanied me, Hailey Woldt and Jonathan Hayden).

As a professor on campus, I would recommend essential reading to Muslims during our travels and now to you all to help us understand each other: The first book is by my friend, Dr. Jonathan Sacks, the Chief Rabbi of the United Kingdom, and it is called "The Dignity of Difference." It is a powerful plea for Abrahmic understanding in the age of globalization. The second book I would like to recommend is also by a friend, Karen Armstrong, and her book is "The Battle for God." In this book, Karen illustrates how the three different faiths Judaism, Christianity, and Islam, are all going through a period of intense internal debate in which what she calls the "fundamentalists" who are in opposition to the more "moderate" or "liberal" versions of faith. The third is my own book, "Islam Under Siege," which argues that we are living in a world in which societies are all feeling under siege. When societies are under siege they tend to be defensive and there is little scope for wisdom and compassion.

Essentially, I have one recommendation, one that can easily be dismissed as too idealistic, but that is the only way to making a lasting peace for the United States and the Muslim world: It is to create friendships across religion, race, and tradition. I have discovered that once friendship develops then everything can change. Without these friendships, dialog itself remains a restricted exchange of ideas and leads to little else. This suggestion may be unlikely, but without genuine friendships forming, we cannot expect any major changes in how we are dealing with the political situations on the ground. Take the example of the Palestinians and the Israelis. Too often the two view each other as enemies and are not prepared to concede anything except in terms of an advantage to themselves. The result is that even if there are concessions there are seen to be a result of bitter negotiations which continue to leave acrimony on both sides. But if both parties are able to create friendships and then meet as friends, the situation will be very different and the peace process itself may take on a new momentum and a new meaning.

In conclusion, this will not be easy, but the exercise to understand the Muslim world is not a luxury for the United States—it is an imperative. It is the first step to confronting the looming series of world crises, and as you on the panel are those who this great Nation looks to for wisdom and guidance, I plead with you to set aside the partisan and parochial issues to focus on the challenges of providing justice, compassion, and friendship in this dangerous, uncertain, and violent time.

The CHAIRMAN. Well, thank you very, very much, Mr. Ahmed.

And now we call upon Dr. Khan for his testimony.

STATEMENT OF DR. MUQTEDAR KHAN, ASSISTANT PROFESSOR, POLITICAL SCIENCE AND INTERNATIONAL RELATIONS, UNIVERSITY OF DELAWARE, NEWARK, DE

Dr. KHAN. In the name of God, most merciful, most benevolent. Distinguished chairman, Senator Lugar, and Senator Boxer, it is indeed an honor to share my expertise with this august body. As I was sitting here, I was thinking of an important Islamic ritual called shura, and I think we practice shura with great nobility and distinction here in the United States and in any Muslim society, unfortunately. Shura means the process of consultation and deliberation.

Islam is structurally a dynamic religion that is systemologically pluralistic from the very beginning. What I mean by structurally dynamic isn't bad, that it has internal mechanisms that allow it to be continuously evolving, to be reinterpreted, and as a result of its internal dynamic structure Islam continues to remain relevant to Muslim life regardless of time and place. It is not a coincidence or an accident that Islam is more meaningful to Muslims, whether they live in the West or whether they live in the East, than other religions in other societies.

But what is also interesting about Islam is its internal pluralism. From the very beginning there have been many interpretations of Islam. It is safe to say that there have been many Islams. There have been the Shia and Sunni, rational and traditional, mystical, philosophical, cultural, and juristic. So in the last 1,400 years we have seen several interpretations of Islam. They have coexisted across time and space.

Lately, for the purposes of U.S. foreign policy, since 9/11 we have been trying to imagine a specific interpretation of Islam as perhaps the designated enemy. Conservative Americans, particularly, and Israelis, try to believe that there is a discrete ideological and institutionalized actor called "radical Islam" and sometimes "radical fundamentalist Islam." That is essentially the problem.

I submit to you that it is a mistake to assume that this is a discrete and coherent entity. For example, increasingly in the last few days as the Lebanon crisis has precipitated, people have equated Hamas, Hezbollah, and al-Qaeda as representative of the same phenomenon.

Al-Qaeda and Hamas are Sunni organizations; Hezbollah is a Shia organization. Hamas is very close to Islamic Brotherhood in its theology and its ideology, whereas Zawahiri, the No. 2 person of al-Qaeda, has written books chastising the Muslim Brotherhood. There is enormous enmity between the Muslim Brotherhood and the Jihadis, and therefore there is no sympathy that al-Qaeda has for Hamas. This is why until now we have not seen al-Qaeda target Israel. What is also interesting is that we have never seen Hamas target the United States.

So it's very important for us to not club everything under the rubric of radical Islam, but that does not mean that there is no such tendency of radical Islam. There are many manifestations of Islam today, but for the purposes of American foreign policy it is important to recognize that there is, yes, a very vicious, very violent, very intolerant interpretation which is out there. But in order to understand that, I submit to you that it is better to look at these various manifestations of Islam in the Muslim world as options.

Today there is a near universal consensus in the Muslim world on three issues: No. 1, that there must be political, social, normative, cultural, economic, and structural change. Nobody wants the Muslim world to remain as it is. Everybody wants change. Muslims are struggling to respond to these challenges of modernity and post-modernity, to the challenges of globalization, and particularly to the challenges, the structural challenges that have emerged as a result of the decolonization process.

No. 2, most Muslims agree that there is no security in Muslim societies. They are victims of terrorism and war. As I heard President Bush repeatedly repeat that Israel has a right to defend itself, I kept amazingly wondering as to how nobody has ever said that even the Lebanese have a right to defend themselves. Muslim insecurity is taken for granted.

There is also a strong consensus that Islam must play a role in the resurgence, the reconstitution, revival of the Muslim world, and therefore you see many different options. The point I am trying to make is this: That Muslims are trying through many ways to cope with modernization and globalization. Radical Islam is one option, and it is not an ideological issue.

If moderate Muslims cannot deliver, then Muslims will abandon that option and seek another option. If our moderate allies in the Middle East will not provide Muslims security, dignity, respect, and freedom, then they will turn to the next option. So the United States, when it chooses partners, it is not important to choose partners on the basis of what they say or what they believe, but it is important for us to actually shape the outcomes on the ground in the Muslim world.

There is, however, an alternative interpretation of Islam which is a direct challenger of radical Islam. We sometimes call it moderate Islam, or sometimes we call it liberal Islam. Liberal Islam has three or four important strategic merits for the United States and the West, and I will list them for you.

No. 1, liberal Islam is providing an alternative understanding of world political and global reality in order to prevent the perception that war on terror is a war on Islam. No. 2, liberal Muslims have an interpretation of Islam which places Itjihad over jihad. Itjihad is an intellectual exercise for reviving society, the privilege, education, and development, over violence and conflict.

No. 3, the liberal interpretation of Islam advances an idiom that explains the compatibility of liberal values such as tolerance, democracy, and pluralism. Finally, liberal Islam deconstructs the jihadi discourse to expose the extremist tendencies behind their interpretation of Islam, and underscores the more compassionate and rational dimensions of Islam.

It is important for us to understand who is a moderate Muslim. One of the jokes in the Muslim world is that all moderate Muslims have been "Karzai'd" in the sense that they have become like Hamid Karzai, the president of Afghanistan, who has no respect in his own people. And this is very important for us. When we work with moderate Muslims, we ensure that we do not undermine their own legitimacy in the very constituency that they seek to reform and address.

I would also like to talk to you about American Muslims. The 9/11 Commission, to a great extent, exonerated the American Muslims of any direct involvement in the attacks of September 11. American Muslims are very unique because they are very rich in terms of per capita income, perhaps the richest Muslim community in the world. They are also the highest literacy levels.

The American Muslim community, in my opinion, manifests more of liberal Islamic values and has institutionalized them more than any other community anywhere in the rest of the Muslim world. As a result of that, the American Muslim community becomes a natural ally of the United States.

What role can American Muslims play in this war on terror? American Muslims have enormous potential to become an important ally in America's war against extremism. They can discuss threat assessments and threat identification. This is a role that we can play to a great deal.

American Muslims would have provided the administration with a more accurate picture of the potential for threats from within the United States and outside. It is possible that the American Government is unnecessarily spending vast amounts of resources in surveillance of groups and individuals who may not constitute a threat, and may actually be overlooking those who could be problematic. American Muslim input on this subject can be immensely useful. Many U.S. policy makers continue to err in understanding and predicting the behavior of Muslim groups, and the chaos in Iraq is a case in point.

One interesting distinction that I would like to make is the confusion over Hiz-ut-Tahrir and al-Qaeda. For the last 2 years I've been watching experts in Washington, DC, attribute al-Qaeda's tactics to Hiz-ut-Tahrir, which is essentially a nonviolent organization, and attribute Hiz-ut-Tahrir's ideology to al-Qaeda, thereby committing gross errors. These are things that American Muslims, called on to study these movements, can help the administration in understanding.

American Muslims can provide a Muslim face to American foreign policy, and the administration has already realized the enormous benefits of having somebody like Zalmay Khalilzad as Ambassador to Afghanistan and then as Ambassador to Iraq. But only one. I once confronted Under Secretary Karen Hughes and asked her to name the Muslims in her department, and she said there are 22, but she could not name one. That means they were not sufficiently high up for her to be consulting them for policy making.

It is important that American Muslims be part of this administration. The Bush administration could have appointed a number of prominent American Muslim sportsmen who have respect worldwide, such as Hakeem Olajuwon, or even Imams, local indigenous Imams like Imam Hamza Yusuf, to become spokespersons for America and American Muslims.

Another area in which American Muslims can provide assistance is in human intelligence and also in undercover operations. The recent operation in Canada which arrested 18 was essentially because of the work of a moderate Canadian Muslim called Mubin Sheikh.

And, finally, American Muslims can play an important role in counseling the radical Islamic discourse. One important arena where the United States needs its Muslim citizens is in countering the anti-U.S. propaganda. Both Islamists and governmental media have launched a propaganda war against the United States in response to its war on terror. This anti-U.S. media offensive is determined to focus on U.S. foreign policy excesses and failures.

The enormous success of Islam and Muslims within American borders is an asset to America. It is a wonderful story that needs to be told. The very fact that American Muslims are thriving in America is proof positive that America is not against Islam. If America was waging war against Islam, then Muslims in America would have been its first victims. This is an important message which we need.

Finally, I think American Muslims can restore balance to America's foreign policy. To put it bluntly, American foreign policy in the contemporary era has been a colossal failure, and I think even a potential danger to America's security interests. This administration would do well to listen to some moderate Muslim voices in shaping its foreign policy.

And finally, I want to address what the United States can do. The United States must deliberate seriously on what kind of relations it wishes to have with a religion whose adherents constitute nearly 25 percent of the world population and include over 55 countries. Islam is also the fastest growing religion in all sectors of the West—in the United States, in Canada, in Europe, and Australia. Islam is outside and Islam is inside.

The United States and the West must find a way to coexist with Islam without constantly demanding Muslims to abandon Islam. This is a very important issue for Muslims, since many see the United States as waging a war against Islam. This has to be done at every level, including government, media, and education. One statement by the President saying that Islam is a peaceful religion is not enough. It has to be repeated often, again and again.

The United States must not undermine the important role of maintaining positive United States-Muslim relations for short-term goals or for immediate expediencies.

The United States must improve its credibility. It must practice what it preaches, fulfill its promises, and certainly abstain from betraying those who take risks at our behest. If you look at the situation in Lebanon today, the way we have abandoned Lebanon, I am not very sure if in the near future any moderate Muslim will be able to trust the United States and take risks for democracy at the behest of the United States. Muslims in Lebanon and Christians in Lebanon believe that the United States, after marching them down the path toward democracy, has betrayed them.

American Muslims are America's natural allies and the best community when it comes to institutionalization of liberal values. The United States must embrace it and treat it as an asset rather than as a suspect.

The United States has to make goodwill gestures toward the Muslim world, and that does not mean supporting dictators or selling more arms. Cooperation in areas of development, education, and economic empowerment will go a long way. Evenhandedness in its approach to the Muslim world is absolutely necessary. Abandoning it, especially in moments of crisis, is extremely detrimental.

The United States must also rethink its relations with Islamists, and find ways and means to work with the more moderate Islamists who are pro-democracy, in order to empower them and to isolate the radicals. The United States must find a way to deal with the Arab-Israeli conflict that does not undo years of diplomacy and good work on the United States-Islamic relations every time there is a crisis over Israel.

Muslims think that the United States and the West does not value Muslim life and that we do not care for their human rights. The changing of this perception will take a long time, but the United States can begin with Guantanamo, and by recognizing that Muslims too have a right to defend their lives, their property, their territory, and their sovereignty.

U.S. foreign policy since 9/11 has sought security for America and its ally Israel by deliberately undermining the security of the Muslim world through bellicose rhetoric, irresponsible aggressions, and astonishing disregard for Muslim lives. We must realize that we cannot be more secure by making others feel insecure.

There needs to be a paradigm shift in how we think of security. We live in a highly globalized and interdependent world. Islam is outside, Islam is inside. It is important that we think of security for all, including Muslim nations, Muslim societies. This is imperative.

I leave you with this comment: The United States and Muslim relations will remain a critical component of global politics for a long time. They must be repaired and nurtured. There is no other alternative.

Thank you.

[The prepared statement of Dr. Khan follows:]

PREPARED STATEMENT OF DR. MUQTEDAR KHAN, ASSISTANT PROFESSOR, POLITICAL SCIENCE AND INTERNATIONAL RELATIONS, UNIVERSITY OF DELAWARE, NEWARK, DE

In the name of God, most merciful, most benevolent.

Distinguished Chairman, Senator Richard G. Lugar, and eminent members of the Senate Foreign Relations Committee, it is indeed an honor to share my expertise with this august body. We are engaged today in a highly noble Islamic and democratic ritual—Shura—consultation and I thank you for this opportunity.

Islam is structurally a dynamic religion and has always been epistemologically pluralistic. In simple terms Islam has a built-in mechanism for continuous evolution, reform, and self-rejuvenation through the engine of Ijtihad. Ijtihad is a legal tool that enables Muslim jurists to think independently on issues where scriptures are either silent or ambiguous. It is also a divine invitation to all Muslims and all human beings to think, reflect, and deliberate on God's message and global realities in order to act in the most gracious, most compassionate, and most just fashion. Ijtihad will always keep Islam relevant and meaningful to Muslims and others who are fortunate to be blessed with its grace.

Muslims have from the earliest period, after the death of the Prophet of Islam [pbuh], interpreted Islam in many ways. There have been many interpretations of what the Islamic Shariah—the essence of Islamic message—constitutes, some even contradictory, but Muslims have recognized difference and diversity as a consequence of divine purpose and developed a culture of tolerance for different manifestations and interpretations of Islam.

So from the very beginning there have been different interpretations of Islam, Shia and Sunni, rational and traditional, mystical and philosophical, cultural and juristic. So it is more accurate to talk about Islams rather than Islam. For academic as well as strategic purposes, it is absolutely necessary to distinguish between different Islams and not paint with a broad brush for it will inevitably lead to bad analysis and bad policy.

For the purposes of U.S. foreign policy however, it is important to distinguish between two broad competing historical tendencies within Islamic history. These two tendencies can be captured as a defensive mechanism that seeks to conserve, preserve, and defend "Islam," and eventually leads to narrow, combative, and often intolerant interpretations of Islam and who a good Muslim is. In our times we associate this tendency very strongly with Salafi and Wahhabi groups. But we must be careful to recognize that religious intolerance does not necessarily lead to political confrontation, violence, terrorism, and anti-Americanism. While al-Qaeda is definitely Salafi-Wahhabi and is our enemy, the Saudi royal family and the Qataris and the Kuwaitis are also mostly Salafi-Wahhabis, but they are our friends and allies. Most jihadis are theologically Salafi-Wahhabis, but very few Salafi-Wahhabis are jihadis.

The alternative is a more liberal and compassionate, even mystical interpretation of Islam, which is highly accommodating of difference within Islam and between religions. It is compatible with democracy, religious pluralism, and is often referred to as liberal Islam and or moderate Islam.

WHAT IS RADICAL ISLAM?

Since September 11, there has been a strong tendency among conservative Americans and Israelis to construct the enemy as a discrete, ideological, and institutionalized actor called radical Islam, and sometimes radical fundamentalist fascist Islam. Radical Islam is imagined as a manifestation of Islam that is narrow, intolerant, authoritarian, violent, anti-west, anti-democracy, anti-American and anti-Israel. I too have been guilty of this generalization in an article for current History in 2006. However, since then I have noticed anomalies. Secular, progressive Muslims also often share several of these characteristics with radical Islamists and there is no definitive relationship between conservative and traditional Islam, anti-Americanism, and violence.

There is no doubt that there is at present a very angry and viscous and growing tendency within the Muslim world, but it may be a mistake to put it in a box called radical Islam. For example, Hezbollah and Hams are very different from each other, the former is Shiite, the later is Sunni, the former is motivated by geopolitics, the latter is struggling for independence. Neither shares theological or political goals with al-Qaeda. For example, Hamas has never targeted the United States. Also consider the Wahhabis and Salafis, while al-Qaeda sure is anti-America, not all Saudis, Kuwaitis, and Qataris, who share the same theology, are anti-America or even violent.

My humble suggestion is to consider the various trends—political and theological—as options. Today there is nearly a universal consensus in the Muslim world on three issues: (1) That there must be political, social, normative, cultural, economic, and structural change. Muslims are struggling to respond to the challenges of modernity and postmodernity, not to mention the global geopolitical realities of the postcolonial world. (2) Most Muslims agree that there is no security in Muslim societies; they are victims of terrorism and war. (3) There is also a strong consensus that Islam must play a role in the resurgence, reconstitution, revival, development, and transformation of the Muslim world.

I submit to you that all these movements in the Muslim world—secular bathism, Islamism, resurgent Sufism, the calls for Islamic democracy, for liberal democracy and revolution—are all attempts to cope with the relative backwardness of the Muslim world, its tensions with modernity which is driven by western culture, and its inability to secure itself. Islamists like secular and moderate elites have a vision to offer.

The battle of competing visions will not be won through rhetoric and discourse—it must come through delivery. The vision that delivers reform, change, empowerment, and security will win. So far Islamists have done a better job than most in the Arab world, unlike in South Asia and East Asia. Moderate and liberal Muslims can win the battle for the soul of Islam only if they are able to deliver. So far they have failed. So far everyone has failed except for the radical who at least hit back against those whom Muslims perceive as enemies.

Radical Islam is an option that Muslims have turned to, due to the failure of all other ideas and movements to deliver a stable, prosperous, and peaceful state and society for average Muslims.

Radical Muslims also offer an explanation of global politics and recent history that glorifies Islam, privileges Muslim tradition, and sometimes is consistent with a simplistic view of reality. For example, the current crisis in Lebanon goes a long way to convince Muslims that radical Islamists are right when they say that Israel, with the help of the United States, is out to destroy their nations.

Political, military, economic, and intellectual independence from the West has always been the overriding goal of political Islam. However, the failure of Islamists to achieve these goals in nearly a century, in combination with real and perceived injustices committed by America and its allies against Muslims, has engendered an extremely vitriolic hatred of America in the hearts of some Islamists giving birth to radical Islam. I like to refer to these radicals as rogue Islamists, who are willing to do anything, absolutely anything, to destroy America and its power and will to prevent the realization of Islamist goals. Rogue Islamists and their hateful discourses are globalizing anti-Americanism, and in the process undermining the moral fabric of the Muslim world and corrupting the Islam's message of justice, mercy, submission, compassion, and enlightenment, not of war, hatred, and killing.

Radical Islamists are a threat to both America and Islam. Their discourses are corrupting Islam and generating hatred against the West, modernity, America, and other Muslims who disagree with them. Their most powerful weapons are their ideas and their ability to convince Muslims to even give up their lives in order to hurt America, Americans, and American interests. While America seeks security from the attacks by rogue Muslims and needs to reduce anti-Americanism, moderate Muslims who do not subscribe to the Islamists discourse seek to rescue Islam and innocent Muslims from the corrupting influence of rogue Islamist.

A response to rogue Islamists requires a complex strategy that above all must counter and delegitimize the Islamists worldview and discourses and expose their fallacies and the devastating consequences they could bring to Muslims and the world by triggering a long and bloody global conflict between America and the Muslim world.

LIBERAL ISLAM AND ITS STRATEGIC MERITS

It is my contention that the best antidote to radical Islam is liberal Islam. Liberal Islam cannot only challenge radical Islamist worldview using Islam as the foundational idiom and also provide an alternate interpretation of Muslim reality and a more positive vision of the future.

Moderate Muslims have a very idealistic view of the Islamic duty of jihad. They argue, based on a tradition of Prophet Muhammad, that jihad is essentially a struggle to purify the self and to establish social justice. The highest form of jihad, Jihad-e-Akbar (the superior jihad) is struggle against the self to improve and excel in moral and spiritual realm. The lowest form of jihad is the military jihad that is essentially defensive and constrained by strict ethics of engagement. They correctly point out that terrorism, or Hirabah (war against society), is strictly forbidden by Islamic scholars. They, however, do maintain that Muslims can and must struggle for justice and freedom while strictly obeying Islamic and international norms of just warfare. For Muslim moderates, Islam is a religion of peace without being pacifist.

Moderate Muslims are critical of American foreign policy in the Muslim world. They are also critical of the prejudiced view of Islam in the West and, in particular, among the policy elite who are also quite ignorant about Islam and the Muslim world. But Muslim moderates do not blame the United States or the West or modernity for all the problems in the Muslim world. They recognize that the decline of the Islamic civilization preceded colonialism. They are aware that the decay of free and creative thinking in the Muslim world was not caused by Western powers but came about as a result of internal dynamics. Moderate Muslims are critical of the polemics against the West, the rising anti-Semitism and the tendency to blame Israel for everything problematic in the Muslim world and the growing intolerance, sectarianism, and authoritarianism in Muslim societies. Above all, they lament the intellectual decline of the Muslim world.

Moderate Muslims are also engaged in what is now referred to as the "battle for the soul of Islam." They argue that Islam is a message of compassion and peace sent by God in order to civilize humanity and give human existence a transcendent and divine purpose. They are aghast and reject the use of Islam to incite terror, to justify bigotry and to discriminate on the basis of faith, or gender, or ethnicity. They recognize that Islam has been appropriated by political and extremist groups who are using Islam as an ideology to pursue a counter hegemonic agenda, both with the Muslim world and against the rest, especially against the United States. Moderate Muslims acknowledge the global problem created by "rogue Islamists." They insist that the false interpretations of Islam by the jihadis and their crusades are not only creating a global fitna (crisis) but are also corrupting the essence of Islam and worsening the socio-political, economic, and cultural crisis in the Muslim world.

It is in the battle for the soul of Islam that America and liberal Islam share a common strategic goal and that is the systematic dismantling and delegitimization of the discourse coming from rogue Islamists that projects America as an anti-Islam crusader power and Islam as an ideology of hate and violence. It is in the arena interpretation and reinterpretation of global political realities and religious texts and their contemporaneous meanings that the war on terror will be won or lost. It is also in this contested realm that the hearts and minds of Muslims can be won or lost. So far, while moderate Muslims are beginning to have an impact in this battle in America, they are not even an important player in the Muslim world. American policy makers must recognize the strategic value of liberal Islam and promote and protect it.

The interpretive battle the liberal Islam wages is in three arenas:

- Providing an alternative understanding of world political and global realities in order to prevent the perception that the war on terror is a war on Islam.
- Advance a liberal understanding of Islam within the Islamic idiom that explains the compatibility of Islam and liberal values such as tolerance, democracy, and pluralism.
- Deconstruct the jihadi discourse to expose the extremist tendencies behind their interpretation of Islam and underscore the more compassionate and rational dimensions of Islam.

WHO IS A MODERATE MUSLIM?

As one who identifies himself strongly with the idea of a liberal Islam and also advocates moderation in the manifestation and expression of Islamic politics, I believe it is important that we flush out this "religio-political identity."

Muslims, in general, do not like using the term—moderate, progressive, or liberal Muslim, understanding it to indicate an individual who has politically sold out to the "other" side. Others insist that there is no such thing as moderate Islam, or radical Islam; there is "only one Islam"—the true Islam and all other expressions are falsehoods espoused by the munafiqeen (the hypocrites) or the murtads (the apostates). Of course the unstated politics behind this position is, "my interpretation of Islam is obviously the true Islam and anybody who diverges from my position is risking their faith."

In some internal intellectual debates, the term moderate Muslim is used pejoratively to indicate a Muslim who is more secular and less Islamic than the norm, which varies across communities. In America, a moderate Muslim is one who peddles a softer form of Islam, is willing to coexist peacefully with peoples of other faiths and is comfortable with democracy and the separation of politics and religion.

Both Western media and Muslims do a disservice by branding some Muslims as moderate on the basis of their politics. These people should generally be understood as opportunists and self-serving. Most of the moderate regimes in the Muslim world are neither democratic nor manifest the softer side of Islam. That leaves intellectual positions as the criteria for determining who is a moderate Muslim, and especially in comparison to whom, since moderate is a relative term.

I see moderate Muslims as reflective, self-critical, pro-democracy and human rights, and closet secularists. Their secularism is American in nature. That is, they believe in the separation of church and state, but not French; they oppose the exile of religion from the public sphere. But who are they different from and how?

I believe that moderate Muslims are different from militant Muslims even though both of them advocate the establishment of societies whose organizing principle is Islam. The difference between moderate and militant Muslims is in their methodological orientation and in the primordial normative preferences that shape their interpretation of Islam.

For moderate Muslims, Ijtihad is the preferred method of choice for social and political change, and military jihad the last option. For militant Muslims, military jihad is the first option and Ijtihad is not an option at all.

Ijtihad, narrowly understood, is a juristic tool that allows independent reasoning to articulate Islamic law on issues where textual sources are silent. The unstated assumption being when texts have spoken, reason must be silent. But increasingly moderate Muslim intellectuals see Ijtihad as the spirit of Islamic thought that is necessary for the vitality of Islamic ideas and Islamic civilization. Without Ijtihad, Islamic thought and Islamic civilization fall into decay.

For moderate Muslims, Ijtihad is a way of life, which simultaneously allows Islam to reign supreme in the heart and the mind to experience unfettered freedom of thought. A moderate Muslim is therefore one who cherishes freedom of thought while recognizing the existential necessity of faith. She aspires for change, but through the power of mind and not through planting mines.

Moderate Muslims aspire for a society—a city of virtue—that will treat all people with dignity and respect [Quran 17:70]. There will be no room for political or normative intimidation [Quran 2:256]. Individuals will aspire to live an ethical life because they recognize its desirability. Communities will compete in doing good and politics will seek to encourage good and forbid evil [Quran 5:48 and 3:110]. They believe that the internalization of the message of Islam can bring about the social transformation necessary for the establishment of the virtuous city. The only arena in which moderate Muslims permit excess is in idealism.

The Quran advocates moderation [2:143] and extols the virtues of the straight path [1:1–7]. For moderate Muslims the middle ground, the common humanity of all, is the straightest path.

It is my contention that the mainstream American Muslim community broadly qualifies as an example of liberal and moderate Islam. They believe in democracy, human rights, respect women's roles in the public sphere, and most importantly believe, practice, and advocate religious pluralism.

WHAT ROLE CAN AMERICAN MUSLIMS PLAY IN THE WAR ON TERROR?

American Muslims have an enormous potential to become an important ally in America's war against extremism. If consulted and brought into counterterrorism planning they can help America become more effective, more focused, and more cost-effective. These are the following areas in which they can and could have played a major role:

Threat assessments and threat identification

American Muslims would have provided the administration with a more accurate picture of the potential for threats from within the United States. Their analysis would have helped in making the Department of Homeland Security a vastly smaller and more effective institution.

It is possible that the American Government is unnecessarily spending vast amounts of resources in surveillance of groups and individuals who may not constitute threat and may actually be overlooking those who could be problematic. American Muslim input on this subject can be immensely useful.

Many United States policy makers continue to err in understanding and predicting the behavior of Muslim groups and the chaos in Iraq is a case in point. If American Muslims were involved in the management of Iraq after the war, it would have been easier for Washington to establish better communications and perhaps gain more cooperation from various groups.

Provide a Muslim face to America

American Muslims could have given a Muslim face to America's response to September 11, and the feeling in the Muslim world that this is a Christian-Zionist crusade against Islam would have been averted.

The Bush administration should have appointed a number of prominent American Muslim sportsmen, such as Hakeem Olajuwon, and some Imams such as Imam Hamza Yusuf (American convert to Islam who is well respected in the Muslim world) as special envoys of goodwill to the Muslim world. The State Department is now attempting this in a less prominent way. Prominent Muslim presence in America's diplomatic and counterterrorism endeavors would have gone a long way in not only preempting the rise of anti-Americanism, but also in building trust between America and the Muslim world.

Human intelligence

The most important assets that American Muslims can bring to the war on terror is human intelligence, cultural insights, linguistic skills, and experience and awareness of the diversity within Islamic groups and movements. It is possible that FBI, CIA, and the NSA can access this resource through recruitment. But voluntary support in this area from the community can be priceless.

Many American Muslim scholars have argued that Islam and democracy are compatible. The Bush administration could have recruited several of them to make this case in Iraq and help design the Iraqi democracy and write its constitution. Without a significant input from respectable Muslim scholars, the Iraqi constitution may not stand up to accusations that it is un-Islamic and written to make Iraq subservient to American interests.

Moderate Muslims opposed to extremism can also play a role in undercover operations like that played by Mubin Sheikh in Canada and in the Showtime serial, Sleeper Cell.

Counter-Islamic discourse

One important arena where the United States needs its Muslim citizens is in countering the anti-U.S. propaganda. Both Islamists and governmental media have launched a propaganda war against the United States in response to its war on terror. This anti-U.S. media offensive is determined to focus on U.S. foreign policy excesses and failures. It also seeks to explain every aspect of American policy as if it is serving only Israeli interests. With American Muslims as spokespersons surfing the media and the airwaves in the Muslim world, the United States could have a better chance of getting a more balanced view of its policies.

American Muslims can also counter the abuse of Islam by rogue Islamists and undermine their legitimacy. American Muslim scholars have consistently maintained that Hirabah (terrorism) is not jihad and is strictly prohibited by Islamic principles. They have also demonstrated how suicide bombings violate Islamic ethics of self-defense and are not legitimate instruments of jihad. If the voice of American Muslim scholars was given more attention, say through a White House-sponsored conference on jihad, many of the moderate and liberal elements in the Muslim world would recognize the fallacies in the Islamic edicts of rogue Islamists and the scholars who support and justify their cause.

Restore balance to America's foreign policy

To put it bluntly, American foreign policy lately has been a colossal failure and even potentially dangerous to America's interests. This administration would do well to listen to some moderate Muslim voices in shaping its foreign policy objectives and in determining tactics. Except in the case of Israel, American Muslims have the same vision for the Muslim world as claimed by this administration. American Muslims, too, want wholesale regime changes and establishment of democracy in the entire Muslim world. They, too, want to see the general human rights environment improving and wish that prosperity and freedom would take root in the Muslim world. The difference is that American Muslims would recommend strategies that are more humane and involve less bombing and killing. This administration needs American Muslims and it is time it acted on this need and included them in its policy deliberations.

WHAT CAN THE UNITED STATES DO?

The United States must deliberate seriously on what kind of relations it wishes to have with a religion whose adherents constitute nearly 25 percent of the world's population and include over 55 countries. Islam is also the fastest growing religion in all sectors of the West, United States and Canada, Europe and Australia. Islam is outside and inside, the United States and the West must find a way to coexist with Islam without constantly demanding Muslims to abandon Islam. This is a very important issue for Muslims since many see the United States as waging a war against Islam itself. This has to be done at every level including government, media, and education.

The United States must not undermine the important goal of maintaining positive United States-Muslim relations for short-term goals or for immediate expediencies.

The United States must improve its credibility. It must practice what it preaches, fulfill its promises, and certainly abstain from betraying those who take risks at its behest and when motivated by it to pursue democratization or social liberalization. After watching the way we have handled the crisis in Lebanon and repeated requests for help from the Lebanese Prime Minister, I am not sure anyone will be eager to trust the United States in the near future.

American Muslims are America's natural allies and the best community when it comes to institutionalization of liberal Islamic values. The United States must embrace it and treat it as an asset rather than as a suspect.

The United States has to make goodwill gestures toward the Muslim world, and that does not mean support dictators or sell more arms. Cooperation in areas of development, education, and economic empowerment will go a long way.

Evenhandedness in its approach to the Muslim world is absolutely necessary. Abandoning it, especially in moments of crisis, is extremely detrimental.

The United States must rethink its relations with the Islamists and find ways and means to work with moderate Islamists in order to empower them and isolate the radicals.

The United States must find a way to deal with the Arab-Israeli conflict that does not undo years of diplomacy and good work on the United States-Islamic relations every time there is a crisis with Israel.

Muslims think that the United States and the West does not value Muslim life and do not care for their human rights. The changing of this perception will take a long time but the United States can begin with Guantanamo and by recognizing that Muslims, too, have a right to defend their lives, property, and territory.

United States foreign policy since 9/11 has sought security for America and its ally, Israel, by deliberately undermining the security of the Muslim world through bellicose rhetoric, irresponsible aggressions, and astonishing disregard for Muslim lives. The United States must realize that they cannot feel more secure by making others feel insecure. It is important that the United States work for the security of all, including Muslim nations. This is imperative.

United States-Muslim relations will remain a critical component of global politics for a long time. They must be repaired and nurtured. There is no other alternative.

The CHAIRMAN. Thank you very much, Dr. Khan. Let me say we really appreciate the comprehensive testimony of all four of you, and I know that Senator Boxer and I both have a number of questions. I would like to call upon Senator Boxer first of all, in case she has a time requirement, if you would proceed.

Senator BOXER. Thank you. I do, and I so appreciate that, Mr. Chairman. I found all of you very interesting, and I want to make a few comments here and ask a few questions. How much time would I have?

The CHAIRMAN. Take the time that you require.

Senator BOXER. Thank you. Thank you very much. I'll try to keep it succinct.

First of all I want to say, Dr. Khan, I really liked your idea of having Muslim Americans playing a large role in our foreign policy, especially these days. It just makes sense, and I think we all need to pay attention to that.

The beauty of our country is that we are so diverse, and you're right, the American dream is there for everyone. That's why we are here, to make sure that stays that way, and everyone who has had the opportunity I think could be a great voice for our country. So that I really like.

The place I really disagree with you is your comment about how America has abandoned Lebanon, and I know this is a very hot topic right now, but I feel I must say that as I look at the situation, it isn't America who has abandoned Lebanon, but in fact it is Syria and Hezbollah and the fact that the Lebanese don't have the ability, the wherewithal, to police their own southern border. This is a crisis of major proportions, and if everyone paid attention to U.N. Resolution 1559 and Lebanon could in fact be free of this militia in the south and free of foreign influence, the world would be a far safer place.

Now, I know this is a hot topic. I'm not going to get in an argument with you, but I don't believe in any way that America has abandoned Lebanon. Now, the one way I think America could have done better all these years is to pay more attention to that whole situation, to be pushing so that in fact U.N. Resolution 1559 was listened to, and to play a bigger role in the Palestinian-Israeli conflict. For sure I agree on that, but I don't think in this case you can point to America as the culprit for what is happening there.

And I want to say to His Excellency Ahmed that I so appreciate your insights on religion. For myself, in my youth, I will never forget this because when you're a child and your parents are everything to you, my parents bought me a book. It was called "One God." "One God." And I never forgot it because it was so interesting to me, because the point of the book—it's written for children—was that in essence, regardless of what religion we follow, there is one God at the end of the day.

And that very simple point really unites all people, and I think that unfortunately what has happened with religions, with organized religion over the years is, instead of all of us working on that concept, somehow the differences have come to the fore. And that's a way bigger question than we have time to go into, but I just really think that simple message has to get to children and get to all of us because it will in fact bring us together.

I need to get a few things off my mind here. When I listened to Mr. Kohut and his exceptional work out in the field, he is a bearer of bad news. He doesn't relish telling us this news, but the fact is that the opinion of this country in the world, and frankly if you even look beyond the Middle East, but in the Middle East, is dismal, and I think it is making us less safe. Anti-Americanism, to quote you, Mr. Kohut, is a global phenomenon.

This news is a blow to the American people. When I remember back—again, you know, we all bring our own experience to the table here—when we were so beloved in the world, and rightly so, I mean, we had a clear sense of what we were about and what our role was in the world. And I think we have lost our way and made a lot of mistakes, and rage toward America makes us less safe and anger makes us less safe.

I personally believe that, you know, you take President Bush's urge for democracy and elections, but you couple it with this anger, and what you get is Hamas winning in the Palestinian Territories, and Ahmadinejad being elected in Iran. Even in Iraq the Bush administration favorites lost, and one didn't even get any votes. In other regions of the world the same thing is happening, sadly in our own hemisphere.

So while democracy as a goal is laudable, we have got a lot of homework to do to make sure that we are seen as a success and a beautiful model of what the world should all be like, and it's just not happening out there. I want to talk about why I think that's so, and I don't want to be simplistic about it because it's not simple. Just listening to you, Dr. Hoffman, I mean, it's complicated.

But I think after 9/11 we had the whole world with us, Mr. Chairman. You remember. The whole world. In France the headline was, "We are all Americans." And we blew it by going into Iraq. There wasn't one al-Qaeda cell there on 9/11. I have shown this booklet on many occasions, as has Senator Feingold. This is a State Department document that came out right after 9/11, showed where al-Qaeda was. Not in Iraq, no way, not one cell. Not one cell in Iraq.

But instead of going after Osama bin Laden who attacked us, keeping it clear, keeping the world together, going after terrorism, we turn around on a dime and we go into a place where our own State Department said there wasn't one al-Qaeda cell. And the President still said Iraq is part of the war on terror, and he said it at the time, and the fact is, the terrorists moved in there after we went in there, because we became real fuel for the insurgency.

We are sitting ducks. We're losing. I read today that yesterday we lost another five Americans, Mr. Chairman. About 23 to 25 percent of the people we've lost over there, of our military are either from California or based in California. It's extremely painful. I think the war in Iraq is a gift to Osama bin Laden, and it's a gift that keeps on giving every day that we are there. It's fueling the recruitment of terror groups, the more we get bogged down. And as I said, now al-Qaeda in Iraq is there, and they're responsible for 10 percent of the violence there, the most heinous violence.

So I have a question here about a comment by Peter Bergen, and I'm going to address it to Dr. Hoffman. Peter Bergen, as you all know, I think most of you know, is an expert on terrorism. He said, "What we've done in Iraq is what bin Laden could not have hoped for in his wildest dreams." This is all his quote. "We invaded an oil-rich Muslim nation in the heart of the Middle East, the very type of imperial adventure bin Laden has long predicted was the United States' long-term goal in the region."

Dr. Hoffman, do you agree with Peter Bergen that the war in Iraq played right into the hands of Osama bin Laden and those who are twisting the Muslim religion to benefit the war on terror?

Dr. HOFFMAN. Yes, I do. Certainly in bin Laden's seminal thoughts, which I referred to in my testimony, that was issued in August 1996, in fact in the last pages he predicted that the United States and the United Kingdom would use Saudi Arabia as a base to wage a predatory and aggressive campaign against Islam, with the intention of taking over the Muslims' most precious natural resource, the oil in the region. So in some respects he was cuing this up long before it occurred.

The reason though I agree with Peter is that there was an enormous change in al-Qaeda's propaganda in February and early March 2003, where the more ideological statements that appeared on alneda.com, its principal Internet organ then, were replaced by actual clarion calls to battle, calling upon jihadis to converge on Iraq to resist this latest instance of Western aggression; not to prop up Saddam Hussein but rather to use this as an opportunity, I think an opportunity that they had lost because of their defeat in Afghanistan, to confront United States forces and to use suicide terrorist tactics and other means. So certainly I think it did play into his hands, that this was one of the battlefields that he sought to create.

By the same token, though, I think today we are in an enormously difficult situation where immediate withdrawal is not a solution, because this would indeed also play into his hands, in the sense that this would be trumpeted, much like the withdrawal of the Soviet Union from Afghanistan in 1989, as yet another victory for the jihadi terrorists, and indeed perhaps even add more fuel to the fire in their aggressive intentions.

Senator BOXER. Well, you have said it well. The worst leadership—you didn't say this—to me the worst leadership is when you have no good choices. You know, as a mom I always learned from the child psychologists that you give your kids three good choices before—you know, you say, "You can either go to bed at 8:00, 8:15, or 8:30." You know, they are all good choices.

Well, we don't have a good choice. Either we leave and cut our losses, or we stay, continue our losses, because we're not sure what's going to happen. It could be used as propaganda and the rest. That's a debate that we're having here every single day and every single minute, really, within the parties and across party lines. But to me the fact is, you never can forget why you're in this situation if you're going to be able to have better policies in the future.

I have one last question, if I might. You have been so kind and generous, Mr. Chairman. I really appreciate it.

You know, again on the dilemma that you pose, get out or stay, I was thinking the other day, if each of us picture ourselves in a room with a swarm of bees, and the door is shut and we're in the room, and we have insecticide to spray that doesn't work too well but it helps a little bit, we have a newspaper to swat, and then we have the door we could open and get out, I think that reminds me of where we are. However, I do think closing the door is the best option. You could figure out how to deal with the situation once you're safely out of the room.

But again, I'm not asking about that because you fortunately don't have to vote on those kind of issues. I do. And you don't have to write the letters that I write every day—every day—the condolences. So that's where we are.

So I want to go back to public opinion, Mr. Kohut. You found, in a global opinion poll released last month, that favorable views of the United States continue to drop throughout the world—throughout the world. According to your report, "America's global image has again slipped, and support for the war on terror has declined even among close United States allies like Japan. The war in Iraq is a continuing drag on opinions of the United States, not only in predominantly Muslim countries but in Europe and in Asia as well."

I want to ask you first, do you think—you mentioned the war in Iraq. If you were to—I know it's hard for you to do this—put a percentage as to how much of a role the war in Iraq has played in that opinion, and while you're thinking about this, also, do the people in the world know that Americans don't really agree with this administration on Iraq?

Because in March, the Pew Research Center conducted a poll of Americans in which respondents were asked to give a one-word impression of the situation in Iraq. This is in our own country. According to the poll, the words "mess," "bad," "chaos," "terrible," and "disaster" were offered most frequently, along with such variants as "hopeless," "pitiful," "Vietnam," and "out of control."

So do you think the people throughout the world are distinguishing between the American Government's policy in Iraq and the American people and their views? Hard questions, I know.

Mr. KOHUT. Well, I think that probably in the Muslim world that distinction is not being made. There is more convergence between anti-Americanism toward the government and not liking the American people in the Muslim world than elsewhere. Perhaps in Europe there is a greater sense, or among our allies more generally there is a greater sense that there is discontent with the war, although attitudes toward the war in the United States, as you know, remain highly partisan. There is not discontent with the war among Republicans. It's mostly among Democrats and Independents.

So I think the answer is a mixed one to your second question. As to your first question, I would give you the two headlines. In 2002, before the war in Iraq, our headline was that there is growing dislike of the United States around the world and discontent with the United States, but there's still a reserve of goodwill toward the United States all around the world, outside of the Muslim world. A headline in May of 2003, when things were really going pretty well in Iraq, was that the U.S. image has plummeted all around the world, and it pretty much hasn't recovered. There have been some ups and downs.

A lot of what we were writing about this year was the fact that the progress we had seen in some places last year had slipped back, in Indonesia, in India, in Russia, for example. But, you know, the war in Iraq is the 800-pound gorilla with respect to the image of the United States around the world, but perceptions of America's policies with respect to Israel and Palestine, the Israeli-Palestine dispute is the 800-pound gorilla in that realm of the world.

And I wanted to react to the comment you made with respect to Dr. Khan's comment. I think whether the United States has abandoned Lebanon or not, that is probably the perception in the Muslim world today, because in the Muslim world so many people think, even in places like Kuwait where the United States still has a good image, that we unfairly support Israel. So I would think that in that dispute, I would think that what's bad for Israel, what makes Israel look bad in that world among the public, makes us, the United States, look bad.

Senator BOXER. Well, I was heartened to hear some Lebanese saying that it's time Hezbollah got out, and when you look back at the assassination of Hariri, maybe that was a turning point, too. So I think it's a little more complex than just as simply as you lay it out there.

But, Mr. Chairman, I so appreciate this hearing. I know it's not well-attended because of so many competing things going on, but I just have learned a lot, and I so appreciate this panel and your indulgence. Thank you.

The CHAIRMAN. Well, thank you very much, Senator Boxer. I share your enthusiasm for this panel and the timeliness of the hearing. I appreciate so much your presence.

Senator BOXER. It would have been a little more lonely for you, I know.

The CHAIRMAN. Exactly, and we're grateful. And I would just say that Senator Boxer is a regular attendee at our hearings, but nevertheless has, as I do, an intense interest in the issues that we have before us this morning.

Let me begin my questioning by noting that the Aspen Institute, among other good things that it does, has a congressional program, and a study program following 9/11 proceeded to try to bring some instruction to Members of Congress, Senate and House, about Islam. This is sort of basic training for many of us, and this is achieved through breakfast meetings here in the Capitol and likewise through conferences in other countries. So recently we had, at least several of us, 17 as I recall, were in Istanbul for a conference that brought together people from the area as well as scholars from the United States and our own resources.

Now, during these conferences, you mentioned, as I recall, Dr. Ahmed, Karen Armstrong as one of the authors whom you were recommending, and she has participated in our conferences, as have other scholars that you would recognize, and that has been helpful. Whenever any of their books arise, we are alert because we have heard the persons, have had some dialog, in the presence of people who had a variety of Muslim experiences, and that has been important. That's a point that you have made, Dr. Khan, as well as you, Dr. Ahmed.

Let me just say that having said that, one of the themes of the early conferences came down to this thought, whether it's a 200-year separation and problem or whatever the time frame, that the Industrial Revolution proceeded in Europe and did not proceed, at least in the same form, in the Muslim world; that essentially Europeans, because of the modernity or what have you that came from the Industrial Revolution, gained wealth, gained substantial capital, and that did not occur in many states in the Middle East.

And, furthermore, there were different developments in attitudes toward women. In the most stark sense, Europeans would say we utilized the total work force, and in some Arab and Muslim states people would say we used half of the work force; women were not a part of this. Now, that overgeneralizes the situation, but nevertheless there were very stark differences in attitude.

So, as a result, at the end of the day, whether this is for good or for bad, a number of countries that appear to be in the West, in Europe, leaving aside the United States, appear to be doing reasonably well, and a lot of young people coming up in the Middle East do not appear to be doing very well, and they don't have very much hope of doing very well under the current circumstances.

Now, whether that is the basis for problems or not, the fact is that into this picture about 60 years ago—we have learned in other hearings in this committee in which we have discussed energy to a fair-the-well—the United States and Saudi Arabia got together during the Franklin Roosevelt administration. We had mutual interests, and among them, perhaps paramount, was oil and the possibilities that that had for us and for Europe, and ultimately for Japan and for others who were in industrial situations.

There was not necessarily a pact between the two countries, the United States and Saudi Arabia, or any other particular country, but nevertheless it was fairly well understood that those lines of oil were vital to us, as well as the income to the rulers of Saudi Arabia, and as a result we began to take steps to make certain that that continued. One could make a case that when we became heavily involved with the Shahs of Iran we had similar thoughts, but in any event we were involved.

Now, this maybe, for many in Congress became more acute as Iraq invaded Kuwait, and there were prospects that that invasion might proceed right on into Saudi Arabia, into the oil fields there, quite apart from what was occurring in Kuwait. And President Bush, the first President Bush, talked about pushing back aggression. We sought United Nations support to do that.

We also sent as many as 500,000 American troops into the area. We were the only country that could do that, and it was one of the first manifestations of that essential point in world politics, that the United States alone really had that transporting quality, that mobility to tackle difficult problems, and that was one we decided to tackle. The Saudis, after some deliberation, decided that they would like for us to come to their defense and we, in fact, began to put a good number of troops in Saudi Arabia.

Now, after the war, the troops stayed in Saudi Arabia. Some who have testified before our committee, perhaps in less comprehensive form, have indicated that this is not necessarily when we caught the attention of Osama bin Laden. His own history has been a source of considerable interest to the committee from time to time, his earlier beginnings, his work in African states, his work moving through many states, and his relationship with family in Saudi Arabia, for that matter.

The question that I have for all four of you to begin with is a major part of the American predicament, leaving aside any other country, the fact that there is considerable strategic resentment—not simply overall public relations problems but strategic resentment—of American military forces in the area who appear to be there, if not on a permanent basis, at least readily available to get there, given the mobility of modern means, and who have in fact been there on a permanent basis in one form or another, despite destruction of barracks in Saudi Arabia, movement of troops to more secure locations in the course of time, all sorts of allegations as to who really was responsible, whether Iranians were involved, quite apart from persons in the al-Qaeda movement, or indigenous Saudi forces, whoever. This has been a part of our predicament, if not a major part. The United States has a reliance upon oil in that area, as does the rest of the world, and the rest of the world depends upon us to maintain the flow.

As a matter of fact, when for example, 2 months or so ago there was a rumor that terrorist forces, whoever they were, were coming down the road toward a refinery in Saudi Arabia that reportedly produces 13 percent of refined oil in any one day, in which the world has maybe a 2 percent discrepancy between supply and demand, so the knocking out of that sent chaos into the Western world, the good news was, the terrorists were stopped, whoever they were. The Saudis indicated they had security there, but there was a shakeup. Prices of oil spiked. In other words, there was a recognition by the rest of the world that life as we know it in industrial Europe, Japan, and the United States wouldn't come to an end but it would be severely dislocated.

So, as a result, armed forces are required to try to maintain these supply lines. Is there any hope for the reconciliation we're talking about today, or movement, so long as this energy need remains and the United States finds it incumbent to be present to protect our interests and those of others?

I would just add that the first George Bush financed the Kuwait/ Desert Storm situation through a vast international United Way campaign. I happened to be with the President of the United States at that time when he got a call which was vital from the Prime Minister of Japan, informing the President of the first very generous contribution of Japan to this effort, which was followed by several more generous contributions. I really saw diplomacy at work in that way.

Is there, I ask first of you, Dr. Hoffman, a way for reconciliation, goodwill, a better opinion of everybody, quite apart from al-Qaeda being on the march or not on the march, while we are there and while there are vital interests that we feel we need to protect, as well as, for example, Saudi friends?

Dr. HOFFMAN. Well, you know, your question is an excellent one and it's obviously a very complex one. I think you're right, though, that at least historically—we've been examining early al-Qaeda documents at RAND now for the better part of a year—it seems quite clear that bin Laden was no friend of the United States from his formative period in Afghanistan, but it was really the Palestinian-Israeli conflict that was something of a fulminate.

But I think it remained in the back of his mind until Saddam Hussein invaded Kuwait and we had the massive build-up, which on the one hand he thought the United States would never leave the region. On the other hand he also thought, as you were zeroing in on, that this was part of a United States policy to extract from Muslims undervalued oil resources and energy resources, and this became one of his points of contention against the United States.

I think the flash point for his turn to international or global terrorism was the influence of Ayman al-Zawahiri, his No. 2, who is an Egyptian, head of an Egyptian Islamic jihad terrorist group, where he at least began to formulate this concept of a far and a near enemy. And I think it was the failure of al-Zawahiri's group to overthrow the Mubarak regime in Egypt in the early 1990s that influenced bin Laden: Let's not deal with the near enemy, the local powers that the United States props up and supports, but let's move to the puppet master in the back, and that focused on the United States.

In responding to your question, I'm not an energy specialist at all, but I think you're hitting an important nail on the head. And that is, we tend to look at all of these movements as monolithic, and we indeed buy, I think, the terrorist propaganda that they have a united, undivided front directed against us, when in fact I think very much the opposite is the truth, that they are subject to the same divisions, especially the same very acute personality rivalries. I believe Abu Musab al-Zarqawi's rivalry with bin Laden and al-Zawahiri is an example of this.

And I think that we're not as sensitive as we should be, largely as my colleagues on the panel have argued, that because there is, I think, a large amount of our attitude toward the Middle East and toward the Muslim world that's based on conjecture rather than on a deep knowledge, and therefore without this deep knowledge, this understanding, not just in detail, of our adversary, which I think in this conflict is amongst the poorest we have ever faced.

In Vietnam, for example, we encountered many frustrations, but one thing, it cannot be said of the United States effort that we did not understand our adversary in the National Liberation Front, the Vietcong. There were detailed studies and interviews with thousands of Vietcong detainees, so we built up a very clear picture, not just of how they operated and functioned and recruited but of the divisions within their ranks, and then we could direct very, I think, finely calibrated and effective information operations and propaganda to drive even a wider wedge.

So I think on the one hand we haven't taken advantage of this same opportunity with many of the detainees we have in the war on terrorism and in Iraq to really understand our adversary. And I think, as we've heard from my three colleagues on the panel, we fundamentally don't understand the constituency in the Middle East, in the Muslim world, who we need to appeal to, who we need to enlist in the struggle, and rather in recent years we have inadvertently, perhaps, alienated.

The CHAIRMAN. Let me just pick up with Dr. Khan for a moment this point from Dr. Hoffman's testimony. You made a very valid point, for instance with the Karen Hughes operation, that she was not able to identify the Muslims on the staff. Perhaps they were not conspicuous or high up enough.

But it's a more basic problem than that that Karen Hughes has. We, it seems to me, are hamstrung, as we have heard in these hearings, by our own problems of trying to identify people of any of the Muslim situations who are seen as reliable by our Government, to the point for example that if Osama bin Laden were intercepted by the United States on a tape, on cell phone, it is always a question of who would be able to translate what he had to say. Would we know really what the conversation was? Is the data mining sufficient finally, and are there enough people with language ability, interpreters, to try to fathom through this?

Now, we get conflicting testimony. People say, "Well, you have to understand, we do background checks for people involved in intelligence or public relations and so forth, and there are difficult aspects to these background checks. We find unusual people coming into the lives of these people, and therefore what kind of reliance can you put on this sort of thing?" It's a circular thing that goes round and round, through perhaps an ignorance of all the nuances here.

As somebody who has studied this perhaps more carefully than most, how do we begin to get some basis for enlisting people of Muslim faith, moderate or not, who are eager to play a role in the United States Government, to be able to assist us in whatever we are doing now?

Dr. KHAN. Thank you very much. There is a very interesting dilemma that intelligence agencies and the U.S. Government has, and that dilemma is that the most interesting people that will be most useful for the government are people who have interesting contacts back home.

The CHAIRMAN. Yes.

Dr. KHAN. And they are the people that the government suspects the most.

The CHAIRMAN. Interesting histories.

Dr. KHAN. Yes, so we need people who know radical Islamists, who know people who can call up Lebanon and find out whether the Lebanese army is supporting Hezbollah or not. The kind of person who can find that thing out for us is also the kind of person we would like to send to Guantanamo.

Now, that is the whole dilemma for the U.S. Government as to how to resolve this, and I heard that there are going to be changes at the Central Intelligence Agency on recruitment. It's coming down the pipeline. Unfortunately, we have bureaucratic and legal issues which take a long time to come.

But there are also several other issues. I think that U.S.-Muslim relationships have been corrupted by oil to a great extent. It is like dating an exceptionally beautiful person, and what happens is that the physical beauty distracts from all the other qualities of the person. So when we started dating the Middle East, we only focused on oil. We have never seen them as human beings.

The United States has had more closer diplomatic relations with Saudi Arabia than with Israel, but there are no people-to-people relations between the people of Saudi Arabia and the American people. And this whole idea of looking at Islam and even American Muslims through the lens of the Middle East has created invisible barriers.

American Muslims, too, made a big mistake when they became politically active in this country and started trying to participate in this policy. They made the goal of reducing the influence of the Israeli lobby as one of their most important goals, and making the Palestinian cause as their No. 1 goal. It's like a flyweight boxer taking on a heavyweight boxer in their first bout. And as a result of that, the American Muslim community has not been able to approach the government, and has remained a challenge and a critique and not a participant.

And these are the two reasons why, when Karen Hughes comes into this position, she does not know whom to hire and whom not to. I took her with me to the Islamic Society of North America, and there she made this very interesting comment. She said, "You have more credibility than I have in the Muslim world." And then she proceeded to travel to the Muslim world without any Muslims with her on the whole tour. And so I went on radio and I said, "Madam, you left your credibility behind." And this is——

The CHAIRMAN. She left you behind, Dr. Khan.

Dr. KHAN. No. There are two other comments that I wanted to add about your previous question to Dr. Hoffman. I think beyond the Iraq issue there are two or three very clear issues which alienate Muslims from America.

Muslims and Third World countries have always admired America because America in their mind is a colony that made it big, a British colony that made it big. So can India, so can Egypt. So everybody looked up to the United States as a role model for development. But what has happened beyond Iraq, and keeping the Iraq issue aside, is there are three things which have created a lot of resentment against America.

No. 1, Muslims tried in two different ways to develop in the last 50 years. One model was socialism, and it led to dictators like Nassir and Saddam Hussein, and so socialism failed them. The other alternative was Islamization, which never really got going because Muslims have seen the United States as a barrier to Islamization and therefore a barrier to development and modernization.

No. 2 is the Arab-Israeli conflict. The Arab-Israeli conflict has been a source of pain, misery, and humiliation to Muslims all over the place, and that is really important to Muslims. While I was coming for this hearing, a Somalian cab driver was lecturing me on how I would be betraying Islam if I did not raise the Arab-Israeli issue in this Senate hearing, and so I am not betraying Islam. [Laughter.]

No. 3, there is this perception in the Muslim world that the United States now is determined to keep the Muslim world weak, and therefore, while it looks the other way when Israel has nuclear weapons, it's determined to go after Iran which does not have nuclear weapons and prevent it.

So these three perceptions—and it has not to do much with oil, actually—these three perceptions have created a sense of resentment, and I think that there are two things that America can do to reverse this. One is to have a just solution to the Arab-Israeli conflict just now, as quickly as possible. The other is to develop a respect. We need to develop human-to-human contact. People have to know.

When I travel through the Muslim world and listen to a lot of anti-Americanism, I start by saying this. I say, "Did you know that last year Americans gave over $250 billion in charity, in sadaqah, which is nearly twice the annual income of Saudi Arabia?" That stuns them. It completely deconstructs their perception of Americans as immoral, because giving charity is a great, great value in Islam. It changes the way they think. They need to know the softer side of America, and so does America need to know the softer side of Muslims. Oil and Israel prevent us from doing that.

The CHAIRMAN. Well, maybe they do, and I suppose my first question was a suggestion that they do, but for the moment it's not really clear to me how we get away from the oil. This is sort of a passionate cause of my own, and I will not bedraggle the hearing with this, because I think without a very sharp diminishment of the use of oil in this country, we are fated to have the sort of problems we're talking about today indefinitely, and this is simply a fact of life.

As a matter of fact, we have been through the process of talking about Ukraine and Russia and European business with natural gas, but the facts of life increasingly are the strategic use of oil. As Iran becomes more wealthy, leaving aside the Saudis or anybody else, it creates very grave dilemmas for us.

Now, on the other hand, we have a strategic alliance with Israel, an affinity there that is important to most Americans and is not going to go away, not going to diminish. So we make the case again, and perhaps we will have the wisdom for a peace process, for cease-fires, for some diminishment of this, and we all pray that that's the case almost every day, but how, factually, that comes about is hard to come by.

We started our day in the committee hosting the Egyptian Foreign Minister and other ministers that are here for talks on strategy with the United States, and they were tremendously interesting with their insights on the cease-fire or how you begin to separate the parties in Lebanon, quite apart from Syria, quite apart from anyplace else. We always are eager to get advice, but I came away from that meeting not sure if these are problems with regard to public opinion. Beyond that there are simply the emotions; we separate ourselves very rapidly.

Now maybe, as you have suggested, Dr. Khan, if our generosity to countries was more apparent it would have a greater effect. Mr. Kohut has mentioned Indonesia looking a little better, at least those parts of it, I suppose, that were helped after the tsunami, and that would be true in Pakistan, where relief came to people up in the mountains. Clearly, if we were more adept at our public diplomacy—as you have suggested, our generosity to other places in the Middle East has been profound, and so the word needs to get out. We need to be better at this.

But I keep circling around sort of basic problems that are in the way of all of this resolving itself very rapidly.

Dr. KHAN. Let me give you a small suggestion, like for example, who is going to rebuild Lebanon? Do we wait until Iran provides some funding to reconstruct Lebanon? A decision by the United States now to say that once there is cease-fire and Hezbollah is either dismantled or moved away, further away, so they cannot threaten northern Israel, the United States will be willing to reconstruct the damage that Israel made in Lebanon——

The CHAIRMAN. That's probably a good idea, but let me just ask as a matter of practical politics, to any of you, who in the world is governing Lebanon at this point? Even if we were to make these pledges, where is there a government that has enough profound influence throughout all of the precincts of Lebanon that any American statesperson, contractor, soldier, or what have you would be safe in the place?

In other words, as I listened to the Egyptians talking today about rockets in the houses of people in Lebanon, up and down the street and so forth, being utilized by the powers that be that are firing at the Israelis and so forth, I'm not sure, who are the Lebanese? Where is the governance, and where do the Syrians come into this? Are they out of it? Are they into it? Should they be back into it?

In other words, I think your point is well taken, but trying to separate all of the parties here so that we have at least some possibility of doing good is not really clear in my mind. Can anybody else offer some clarity as to how?

Ambassador AHMED. Yes, Mr. Chairman. I wanted to make a comment related to the discussion.

You not only have Lebanon. Turkey has issued a statement that it is now looking at the Kurdish incursions into Turkey and seriously considering going in. India and Pakistan are once again heating up in terms of the rhetoric between the two countries, the two giants, both nuclear, three wars between them.

What Iraq has established is a precedent, and that is so dangerous. The United States in this situation, as the sole superpower, needs to be acting, needs to be thinking three steps before something takes place, rather than reacting. It just cannot afford, it is too big. It is the oil tanker in a small pond.

Now, the situation is that you have got Iraq, you have Iran, Syria being involved, Iran being involved. And in my travels I discovered that a lot of Sunnis—and this is an important nuance in the Muslim world, the Shia-Sunni nuance—a lot of Sunnis were referring to Ahmadinejad as the role model. Now, why? Osama bin Laden, who is a Sunni, is understandable. Simply because he is standing up to the United States.

So the United States needs to be aware of the trend and move ahead of the trend, the graph itself. It cannot wait for events. It cannot say, "Let us see what is happening in Lebanon." Because Turkey may be involved soon. Suppose India now says, "All right, cross-border terrorism, we are crossing into Pakistan." Pakistan is 165 million people, it's nuclear. It will tilt everything that you're doing in that part of the world.

So putting it in the context of the Middle East, and I know that this is a major concern, the oil and the oil links, and Central Asia, both major oil producing zones where the United States does not have the option of cutting and running, it just doesn't, but it does have the option of changing strategy, of playing the game by the rules as they are played in that part of the world, what the British, if you recall, called the "great game."

That part of the world has seen all the great conquerors coming and going, from Alexander to Genghis Khan. We have now the United States Army there, the most powerful army in the world today. What are the rules there? You need to make allies who respect you. You need to have a word which is respected.

Right now there is a feeling, even in the close allies that you have, apart from the governments who may be allies, and I don't know how loyalty would be if aid stopped, but the people certainly feel that the United States is a fair weather friend, that when policy changes they'll just dump you and walk away, as the Afghans felt.

In the 1980s, the Afghans were the most loyal allies of the United States. They fought the war with the United States against the Soviets. One-third of the Afghan population has lost a limb. They were the freedom fighters. In the 1990s, they became the Taliban. Bin Laden is of that generation and from that school, if you like. So the need to keep allies and friends and recognize them, to play a long-term game, these are the rules of the great game.

And, third, to learn to play the game through the culture of honor and respect and tradition, because if we don't honor people, they have the stories of rape. That is crossing the border. And then this talk of jihadists, Osama bin Laden, al-Qaeda, is meaningless. Every Muslim, whether he is orthodox or secular or mystic, is horrified, as indeed is every good Christian or every good Jew, every good secularist even, when rape is committed of the kind that you are hearing emerging from these horror stories.

So if we are conscious of the great game, if our soldiers abroad, diplomats abroad are realizing that this is a long-term game strategy, we cannot opt out of it, because if we pull out, there is a huge vacuum in the Middle East, Central Asia. Think about it, Mr. Chairman. You have two other local superpowers waiting to emerge, Russia and China, both who have played the game for the last two centuries, imperial Russia, imperial China.

And in the 21st century, two decades, three decades down the road, if America is not aware of the game, playing by its strange rules there—they are playing cricket, you are playing baseball, different kinds of rules—and if you cut and run, you may have a situation where in this vacuum you will get powers that may not be friendly to interests that the United States represents. And to me, ultimately what the United States does represent is human rights, democracy, the ideals of the Founding Fathers. That is the vision and the dream we constantly need to come back to and share with the Muslim world. That message, that bridge is not coming across, and that needs to be reinforced.

The CHAIRMAN. I appreciate that statement because it certainly is important in terms of the debate we're having in this country, which you witnessed. We have a fairly large percentage of the public and a fair number of Members of Congress who, as a matter of fact, wouldn't call it cutting and running, but they want to get out.

They would say despite all the obligations you have suggested, even the possibilities of a vacuum being created with Russia and China and all the rest, that as far as they're concerned we have had enough. People don't like us. They are attempting to subvert whatever we have to do, distorting what we believe we are, and they ought to just proceed, do the best they can.

Now, I don't think that side will prevail but I'm not overconfident. In part, a number of our congressional elections, in which all of us will be involved in 16 weeks, are on these sorts of issues in which things are polarized just around those points, so that what we're talking about today does have long-run circumstances, but it also has some short-term volatility in our own politics, leaving aside whatever is happening in the Middle East.

Let me just ask you, Mr. Kohut, you've been pondering over all of this argument for a while, but we would like your counsel as to what you have heard.

Mr. KOHUT. Well, one thing that's clear is that of all the things that you mentioned in your set of questions, that the war in Iraq has made all of this worse. It has poisoned the well. I don't think that, while Osama bin Laden and his ilk had issues with Americans on the ground in Saudi Arabia through the 1990s, that certainly—I shouldn't say certainly—probably wasn't the case in the Muslim world at large. It wasn't the case in Turkey, where we had a very positive image. It wasn't the case in Jordan and in other places.

I think, though, that the presence of American troops in Iraq raises the issue of Americans in the Middle East, and that makes the American presence there more broadly more of an issue. Similarly, while as Dr. Khan said we were seen as dating for purposes of oil, oil is even more—there is even more skepticism about our motives and intentions because of the war in Iraq.

All of these things have just become worse, and increasingly what we see in, I'm not saying the Arab world, the Muslim world, is an us-versus-them phenomenon. And one of the ways that came through is when we did our poll earlier this year about Iran obtaining nuclear weapons, there was tremendous opposition to that idea in the West and most parts of the world, but not really tremendous opposition among Iran's Sunni neighbors. In Egypt, in Jordan, there was mixed opinion, in some respects, for it.

It's a very, very negative situation that will require some dramatic success for the United States in the eyes of the Muslim publics, and what that is I don't know.

The CHAIRMAN. Well, we very much appreciate your testimony and your response to our questions, and we will try to make as complete a committee record of this hearing as we can, because you have said things that are important for all of our colleagues, and perhaps the public as a whole that takes a look at these hearings through the benefit of C–SPAN or however. These are important moments for us, to try to concentrate on what you have to say and to reread it, and to try to think about some of the other sources that you have cited.

So this will not be our concluding hearing on this subject. This is an education process, as I have indicated, for each one of us who needs to know more, needs to be visiting with people such as yourselves, as you are able to give us this time. We certainly thank you for your generosity this morning.

So saying, the hearing is adjourned.

[Whereupon, at 12:05 p.m., the hearing was adjourned.]

○

www.ingramcontent.com/pod-product-compliance
Lightning Source LLC
Chambersburg PA
CBHW080542290526
45790CB00006B/2512